Routledge Revivals

Learning Begins at Home

First published in 1968, *Learning Begins at Home* records an attempt by two researchers to initiate and assess an innovation in a school in a working-class neighbourhood. The influence of parents upon children's achievement is a platitude of education. The vital question is whether schools can become centres for education for adults as well as children, influencing the parents directly, and the children indirectly through the parents. The research reported in this book suggests that it would be worthwhile for teachers to give more of their time to cooperation with parents. This book will be of interest to students of education and sociology.

Learning Begins at Home
A Study of a Junior School and its Parents

Michael Young and Patrick McGeeney

First published in 1968
By Routledge & Kegan Paul Ltd

This edition first published in 2023 by Routledge
4 Park Square, Milton Park, Abingdon, Oxon, OX14 4RN
and by Routledge
605 Third Avenue, New York, NY 10017

Routledge is an imprint of the Taylor & Francis Group, an informa business

© Institute of Community Studies (a division of The Young Foundation), 1968

All rights reserved. No part of this book may be reprinted or reproduced or utilised in any form or by any electronic, mechanical, or other means, now known or hereafter invented, including photocopying and recording, or in any information storage or retrieval system, without permission in writing from the publishers.

Publisher's Note
The publisher has gone to great lengths to ensure the quality of this reprint but points out that some imperfections in the original copies may be apparent.

Disclaimer
The publisher has made every effort to trace copyright holders and welcomes correspondence from those they have been unable to contact.

A Library of Congress record exists under ISBN: 0710061803

ISBN: 978-1-032-55820-2 (hbk)
ISBN: 978-1-003-43244-9 (ebk)
ISBN: 978-1-032-55823-3 (pbk)

Book DOI 10.4324/9781003432449

LEARNING BEGINS AT HOME

A STUDY OF A JUNIOR SCHOOL AND ITS PARENTS

MICHAEL YOUNG
and
PATRICK McGEENEY

Foreword by Lady Plowden

LONDON
ROUTLEDGE & KEGAN PAUL

*First Published 1968
by Routledge & Kegan Paul Ltd.
Broadway House, 68–74 Carter Lane
London, E.C.4*

*Printed in Great Britain
by Cox & Wyman Ltd.
London, Fakenham and Reading*

© *Institute of Community Studies 1968*

*SBN 7100 6180 3(C)
SBN 7100 6159 5(P)*

*No part of this book may be reproduced
in any form without permission from
the publishers, except for the quotation
of brief passages in criticism*

CONTENTS

	FOREWORD *by Lady Plowden*	*page*	vii
1	THE SETTING FOR THE STUDY		1
2	PARENTS' CONTACTS WITH THE SCHOOL		13
3	PARENTS' ATTITUDES BEFORE THE TRIAL		23
4	THE CHANGES IN THE SCHOOL		42
5	IMMIGRANTS		67
6	TESTS OF EDUCATIONAL PERFORMANCE		87
7	CUM PARENTE		107

APPENDICES

1	PSYCHOMETRIC TESTING *by D. N. Turland*	131
2	QUESTIONNAIRE FOR INTERVIEWS	137
3	THE REGRESSION ANALYSIS *by Susannah Brown and Colin Taylor*	144
4	LIST OF REFERENCES	160
	INDEX	163

FOREWORD
by Lady Plowden

'WHAT a wise and good parent would desire for his own children, that a nation must desire for all children.' These words came in the 1931 Report of the Consultative Committee on the Primary School and were quoted in 1967 in the Report of the Central Advisory Council, *Children and Their Primary Schools*. But the 1931 Report described only how the schools run by the nation could be improved. The part that could be played by a 'wise and good' parent in the education of his child was not mentioned.

The 1967 Report, on the other hand, emphasized the importance of the role of the parents and how their attitude to and interest in the education of their child appeared to be the single factor in the circumstances of the home which contributed most to the child's progress at school. Obviously there are many, many parents who do have this interest in all that concerns their child and his future, and there are others who do not. But it is difficult for people to take an active interest in a subject unless they are sufficiently informed about it. How can parents take an active interest in what the child is doing at school, and give the support which is needed, unless they can know and understand what is happening and the reasoning behind it?

Michael Young and Patrick McGeeney describe in this book an attempt which was made to improve the knowledge of parents. This was in a school in the kind of area in which it has too often been thought that parents, owing to their own educational inadequacies and the difficulties of the conditions in which they live, are not particularly interested in

Foreword

the education of their children. The implication sometimes drawn is that they may not have much of educational value to give to their children.

What comes out so strongly in this book is the passionate but impotent interest of so many of these parents. They wanted their child to do well, they wanted to help, but they felt ignorant and did not know how to do so. They welcomed particularly the opportunity for private talks about their child with his teacher. At the end of this trial, after increased contact and the beginning of communication between teacher and parent, there was a small but significant improvement in some of the scores of the children when they were tested.

The immediate value of the work carried out is two-fold. First, it has shown that the majority of parents, even though some may be inarticulate, lacking in formal education and living in a barely tolerable environment, are interested in the educational progress of their children. They are gravely hampered, though, in the practical development of this interest by the lack of real communication, on a basis of equality, with those who teach their children. Second, it marks the beginning of inquiries into what can be done to extend and deepen this communication, and has laid the foundation for further trials and research in this field.

The curriculum in the best of our primary schools today now starts from the interests of the children themselves; it is not fragmented into subjects. Real life to most children is home and its environment. School may well only be an interlude. How can what is learnt in school have relevance if it is too far divorced from the real life of the child, if it does not build on the strengths of the home, or try to compensate for its weaknesses?

I hope that this book will be read by all who are actively concerned with the education of children, whether they be teachers of children or of students in colleges of education, or whether they be administrators or, of course, parents. Understanding the possibilities of genuine communication

Foreword

and partnership between home and school, and the problems to be overcome on both sides, must be developed. The parents, this untapped source of strength to the school, are waiting. In so far as the education of their children is concerned, many more would be 'wise and good' if they were given the opportunity.

I
THE SETTING FOR THE STUDY

'AMONG the public buildings of the Metropolis the London Board Schools occupy a conspicuous place. In every quarter the eye is arrested by their distinctive architecture, as they stand, closest where the need is greatest, each one "like a tall sentinel at his post", keeping watch and ward over the interests of the generation that is to replace our own. The Board school buildings, as befits their purpose, are uniformly handsome, commodious, and for the most part substantial and well arranged. The health and convenience of both children and teachers have been carefully considered, and in the later ones especially have been increasingly secured. They accommodate a little over 443,000 children, and have been erected at a cost of about four and a half millions sterling. Taken as a whole, they may be said fairly to represent the high-water-mark of the public conscience in this country in its relation to the education of the children of the people.'[1]

John Lilburne, built in 1896, is one of the schools referred to by Charles Booth in these terms soon after it was built. Its origin is remembered by some local people who still talk of the Inner London Education Authority as 'the School Board' – in another half century such people may have caught up sufficiently to refer to the 'London County Council'. The building does not look handsome any more. The brick has been darkened by seventy years of soot. The three gates which pierce the high walls, one labelled BOYS,

---

[1] Booth, C., *Life and Labour of the People in London*, First Series: Poverty, Vol. 3, p. 204. For full references see Appendix 4.

The Setting for the Study

one GIRLS and the other TRESPASSERS WILL BE PROSE-CUTED, are pitted by wartime shrapnel. The asphalt apron which passes as a 'playground' could well have been the same then, although not what is in it. The broken netball post must have been new once, the goal uprights painted on the brick wall white and the outdoor stable-door lavatories less smelly. Both are more dated, though, by the changes in aesthetic standards. These buildings were the Hertfordshire schools of their age, stemming from the School Board's architectural competition won by Mr. Roger Smith in 1872.[1] These towering walls somewhere between Queen Anne Dutch[2] and Gothic in style were handsome to the Victorian eye because they seemed sufficiently 'substantial and well arranged' to endure for a thousand years. The spell has certainly held so far. John Lilburne has been solid enough to outlast the transitory L.C.C. as well as the bombs which evidently reduced the next-door building to a ruin which is still there more than a quarter of a century after they fell.

It has now a dreadful permanence. Our canons of comparison are the glass pavilions in the suburbs, schools looking graceful partly because they seem more feminine and also more temporary, as if a high wind might bear them away. Inside, John Lilburne has been brought into line with modern notions. The solid chocolate brown of Victorian institutions, paint that would last because it would never show the marks from grubby fingers, has been replaced by the fashionable short-lived pastel colours, airy blue and yellow on the stairs, cream in the classroom, primrose in the library. Outside, it cannot be altered. It now seems less like a

[1] The competition followed a resolution passed by the Board in 1871, 'That it be an instruction to the School Management Committee to obtain information concerning the Prussian system of class division, with a separate room and a special teacher to each class, and to report to the Board how far it should be desirable, in determining the plans of new school buildings, to keep in view the possibility of the adoption of a similar system in London.' Spalding, T. A. *The Work of the London School Board*.

[2] An influential book (Robson. E. R., *School Architecture*) published in 1874 said that, 'The only really simple brick style available as a foundation is that of the Jameses, Queen Anne and the early Georges.'

The Setting for the Study

'tall sentinel at his post' than a derelict three-deck ship refusing to sink to its last rest. The effect is sharpened by the outside steps leading up to the main doorways into the building. These alone have no permanent look. They are stuck on, like gangplanks that have just been wheeled into place. Could the architect have forgotten until the last moment that some way into the Ark would have to be found for the children?

Booth designated the neighbourhood around the school 'middle-class' and 'well-to-do'. There are not very many such people left. To the south are rows of post-1945 flats – Jonquil House, Honeysuckle House, Laburnum House – mostly built (before the latter-day L.C.C. began to radiate its influence out from Roehampton) in shiny red brick, set off by rain-streaked concrete balconies. The flats are interspersed with new prefabs, other rubbish-littered bomb-sites besides the one next to the school and ramshackle printing works or clothing factories hung with faded notice-boards appealing to young would-be IMPROVERS or PRESSERS to enter their murky rooms. To the north one can see what Booth was talking about. Here are the squares and tree-lined Victorian streets. Once for City clerks and even managers, some of them still have neat railings covered with climbing roses; more have broken fences, incongruous painted doors and peeling stucco. The occasional house is almost falling down – like the one where the Cappers live. 'When the wind blows up the back, the wallpaper balloons and bulges out. If it weren't for that bloody wallpaper the whole house would fall down.' In others, rat-infested basements have been boarded up. All the people around who have lived in the district for any length of time, and one or two of the older teachers who have, if never living there at least got to know it well, referred, when they talked about decline, to these older houses.

The well-to-do have been moving out for many decades now, and in recent years the migration, mostly eastwards to the nearer suburbs and the pavilion schools, has accelerated.

The Setting for the Study

Into their place have come more and more immigrants (defined by us as parents born outside the British Isles, with Cypriots the largest group, followed by West Indians and Italians). Twenty-nine per cent of the children at John Lilburne were on this view 'immigrants'. They have changed the character of the district. Next to the run-down English betting shop, at whose door John Lilburne children sometimes stand waiting for their fathers to emerge, is a Cypriot grocer's full of black olives, red peppers and green West Indian bananas. On a winter night in a grey street one may see strange sights – once, strongly lit, through half-open curtains could be seen a group of five or six coloured men dancing to an ancient but strident gramophone, gesticulating and talking loud enough to be heard, even outdoors, over the high notes of a trumpet. The natives who are left are now mostly manual workers. The largest single group amongst John Lilburne fathers consisted of workers in the distributive trades, followed by those in building, engineering and transport. The rest were a diverse array of postmen, opticians, policemen, printers, clickers, bookmakers, caretakers, garage mechanics, dental technicians, gold blockers and one professor. Fifty-three per cent of the mothers were working, outside the home as well as in it, in the same sort of occupations as their husbands, except that they were generally even less skilled.

The choice of this district and this school for our study was not accidental. We wanted while the Plowden Committee was still sitting to give a preliminary test to two of the proposals which from an early stage in the Plowden proceedings seemed likely to emerge in the eventual report and to give evidence to the Committee before its report was presented.[1] The first proposal was that a more determined effort than ever before should be made to improve education in underprivileged districts. The second was that parents should be linked much more closely to schools than they traditionally have been. Our intention was to tie these two

[1] A very brief summary of this book was included in the Plowden Report.

The Setting for the Study

proposals together into a miniature programme for one school, and then try it out in practice.

John Lilburne seemed suitable enough for the purpose. There can be no hard-and-fast definition of an underprivileged district. There is always going to be some muzziness about the boundaries of an Educational Priority Area – to use the term Plowden finally adopted.[1] But John Lilburne at any rate seemed to us to be in the sort of district which the Newsom Committee[2] had earlier had in mind when it called for more opportunity for 'pupils of average or less than average ability', and which Plowden later featured. Influenced by what had been done before in the United States, the plea of the Report was for such 'positive discrimination' in favour of the underprivileged as would make the schools they attended first equal to those elsewhere and then better.

But why in such a place rest any hope in parents? Most of the measures that Plowden proposed for E.P.A.s are more straightforward than that. It is obvious they need more and better-paid teachers; more teachers' aides; more nursery schools; teachers' centres for in-service training; extra books and equipment; better buildings; special links with Colleges of Education. Should a special effort also be made in such places to involve parents? Are they not likely to be rather apathetic, if not resistant to any approach from the school? We were not convinced by the objections – rather the reverse. It seemed to us that if parents were not brought into partnership with the schools in E.P.A.s, or anywhere else for that matter, a chance was going to be lost. There was also a very practical advantage in going for parents. On hardly any of the measures we have listed for E.P.A.s, from better buildings to more teachers, could a voluntary body like a research institute take the initiative. We could plead with the authorities to re-order their priorities and to give more to the people in greatest need. We could talk; we could not act. The cost of doing anything was too large for all

---

[1] Central Advisory Council for Education, *Children and their Primary Schools*.
[2] Central Advisory Council for Education, *Half Our Future*.

The Setting for the Study

except an official body, and this even for a limited experiment. With parents the situation was different. The cost of a small trial was not beyond the resources that a research institute could muster, and yet if we were right the gains to the children might be large. For a small investment, which is all that was possible, there was some chance of a big return.

Backing for common sense

Why this conclusion? We should try to explain. Every teacher knows in a general way how great is the influence of the home. If a child comes from a supportive home he is more likely to do well at school, and if from one that is not, he will do less well. It is bound to be so. The child is in the home, and the home alone, for the first vital years of his life, and after he goes to school he is only there for a part of his time. As Burt said in one of his classic reports

> 'Two months in every year, two days in every week and all except five hours out of every day, are spent by the child not at school but somewhere else – at home, in the street, or wherever he takes his recreation.'[1]

The relevance of this commonsensical view to educational policy has become very much apparent in recent years. Each in a choir of major official reports – *Early Leaving,* Crowther, Robbins, Newsom and the latest, Plowden – and a myriad supporting investigators have voiced the same refrain about children whose fathers are in manual occupations. By and large they do not fare so well at school as others, even when like for like in ability. But why? Knowledge is still very incomplete. The father's job is only the reference point. Achievement goes with certain kinds of home and family. The quality of housing matters. The better the housing, the better the children's chances.[2] Income matters,[3] and so above

[1] Burt, C., *The Backward Child,* p. 118.
[2] Douglas, J. W. B., *The Home and the School.* Also Glass, R., *The Social Background of a Plan; a survey of Middlesbrough.*
[3] Fraser, E., *Home Environment and the School.* There is a discussion of the wider influence of working-class values in Young, M., *Innovation and Research in Education,* Chapter 4.

The Setting for the Study

all do the bevy of influences that can be labelled 'parental attitudes'.

There are different ways of measuring them. Douglas, adopting as his criteria the number of visits parents paid to the school and teachers' estimates of the amount of interest the parents showed, found a marked correlation with the children's educational performance.[1] Plowden made use of a much larger number of indices, parents themselves being asked whether, for instance, they spent time with their children in the evenings and gave them help with their school-work, whether they had attended open days and talked with the staff at school, and whether they bought or borrowed books for their children to read. By such means the large part played by parental attitudes can be illustrated; they seemed to be crucial to the children's progress. Common sense of course – but common sense that can be given a new edge by research.

The implication for policy also seemed to us obvious. If an effort is to be made to raise the quality of education in E.P.A.s, however much is done to bring in more teachers and to get rid of the stable-door lavatories in schools like John Lilburne, it will lose in effectiveness unless the co-operation of the parents is won. Teachers can do a great deal for the children when they are at school; they should also be able to do a great deal for them at one remove if they can persuade the parents to take a greater interest in their education, or show their interest, where it already exists, in a more effective manner. In the words of Plowden, 'Schools can exercise their influence not only directly upon children but also indirectly through their relationships with parents.'[2] The moral is a general one, applying to every school in the country; but the general has particular force in run-down districts where children are liable to be most in need of more parental support than they get.

---

[1] Douglas, J. W. B., op. cit.
[2] Central Advisory Council for Education, *Children and their Primary Schools*, p. 36.

The Setting for the Study

Which cause, which effect?

This was the main reason it seemed worth making an attempt at 'action research'. There was another reason too. The line of survey research we have referred to has gone almost as far as it can. Surveys can ordinarily only reveal associations, not causes, although to be of use to teachers it is causes that one wants to understand. There is an association, as we have seen, between parental attitudes and educational performance – but which is cause, and which effect? It may be that parents take more interest in their children because they are doing well, rather than the other way round. The children may be more rewarding and reflect more credit on their parents. Parents respond to the children, and the way their ability declares itself, as well as children to the parents. The sensible way to look at it is not as a one-way affair but as an interaction or, in other words, as a mutual adjustment of expectations and performance which could best be investigated by an intensive study of the same families over time. Bernstein has begun to show how parents influence their children's modes of thinking, long before school is reached, not just by their vocabulary but by the way they use it.[1] Short of further work of that sort, action research of the kind we have broached may at least throw a little light on the extent to which teachers can persuade parents to change their attitudes, and the extent to which, if they succeed, changes are produced in the children.

We did not expect it would be easy to effect any change, especially in a short time, and next to impossible to measure the results of any alteration that was achieved. Children are relatively amenable to persuasion, or education as it is called; adults much less so. There is not a great deal of evidence to show that adults can be persuaded even to stop buying one product and take in another instead, that is where the change is of a comparatively trivial kind,[2] and in

---

[1] Bernstein, B., 'Social Class & Linguistic Development', in Halsey, A. H., Floud, J. and Anderson, C. A, *Education, Economy and Society*.
[2] Katz, E. and Lazarsfeld, P. F., *Personal Influence*.

8

The Setting for the Study

their capacity as voters they are hardly more open to influence.[1] Where attitudes are deeply held, 'conversion' is rare,[2] particularly when people remain in groups and in circumstances which constantly reinforce those attitudes. No far-reaching results could therefore be anticipated, particularly as there was a double task, to persuade teachers first and parents second. If indeed the goal had been to persuade either teacher or parent to change well-entrenched attitudes, it would barely have been worth trying. The project would only be feasible if the attitudes were already relatively favourable to it – with teachers and parents both ready to achieve a higher degree of co-operation once the opportunity was presented – and the object of an initial survey made before any action was taken in the school was to discover whether there was such a readiness, and if so what was it a readiness for.

Obstacle to experiment

We wanted so far as we could to measure the effects upon the educational 'performance' of what was done to involve the parents. We have in fact reported, especially in Chapter 6, the results of some tests given to the children. But we knew that whatever we did it could be no more than a pilot which might lead the way to an experiment as much controlled as experiments with people can be. The main reason was that we were in this work acting more as innovators than researchers. We modelled ourselves to some extent on those teachers (whether associated with the Nuffield Foundation or not) who have developed new methods of teaching mathematics or science or languages, except that our purpose was not to modernize the curriculum but to help work out some arrangements whereby parents could be linked more closely to schools than they often are. Without trial and error we could not know what 'package' of recommendations

[1] Lazarsfeld, P. F. and others, *The People's Choice*.
[2] Klapper, J. T., *The Effects of Mass Communication*.

The Setting for the Study

we would put forward. It followed that an experiment, strictly defined, had to be ruled out. The kind of design needed for this purpose has been discussed many times before.[1] A sample of experimental schools (in the plural) is required, together with a sample of control schools. If the influence of enthusiasm alone is to some extent to be measured, the control schools should if possible be divided into two, those where efforts are made to generate enthusiasm on the part of the teachers for showing off the merits of the *status quo*, and those where no such efforts are made. But this design is impracticable unless there is a more or less standard set of changes which can be adopted in all the experimental schools, each doing much the same as the other, so that some generalization can be drawn about the effect of the same change in many schools. We had when we began this work no such standard changes to propose with any confidence. We had no alternative but to make a case study, and rather than try out different ideas in different schools it seemed better to concentrate for the most part on the one we have described at the beginning of this chapter. We say case study in one school rather than experiment because an experimental group of individual children cannot properly be picked out and compared with a control group of children within one school. There is within one set of walls too much 'contagion effect', the teachers of the control children being liable to be too much influenced by what the teachers of the experimental children do. This is not to say that it is worthless to compare children within a school, as we shall show in Chapter 6.

A case study such as the one reported here has another function too, that is to encourage other Heads to co-operate in further investigations. When we started it would probably have been impossible to persuade large numbers of Heads to

[1] See, for instance, Young, M., op cit. An admirable instance of an educational experiment which goes some way to disproving the common assertion that the experimental method is not open to the social sciences as it is to the natural sciences is reported in Downing, J., *The I.T.A. Symposium*, and other papers on the same subject by Downing and his colleagues.

The Setting for the Study

allow their schools to form up in large samples. But once a case study has been made without too negative a result, it becomes easier to proceed on a more ambitious scale. This case study is now being followed up in several schools by one of the authors (Patrick McGeeney).

Our inquiry was made as usual in a number of stages. We started in a preparatory way to gain experience in another primary school near to, and in many ways similar to, John Lilburne, and we have to some extent drawn for background on the interviews with the parents in that school. In John Lilburne itself we drew a sample of one quarter, or 128, of the children in the junior school, and succeeded in interviewing 119 of their parents, 109 of whom were mothers, and four of whose husbands were also present; the rest were fathers only. The purpose was to find out what their contacts were with the school before any changes were made, and to get ideas from them about the sort of changes that would be acceptable. Chapters 2 and 3 summarize these preliminary interviews. The changes made in the school are outlined in Chapter 4. Some of the special problems of immigrant parents are dealt with in Chapter 5. Changes in the children's educational performance are considered in Chapter 6, and the final chapter is a summing up.

We have many debts to acknowledge.
(1) To Lady Plowden, Stella Duncan, Norah Goddard, Maurice Kogan and other colleagues on the Plowden Committee who provided stimulus and encouragement, as also did Gilbert Peaker, adviser to the Committee on educational research.
(2) To the L.C.C. and to its successor, the I.L.E.A., for allowing us into the schools, and especially to A. Roy Truman of the I.L.E.A. staff. The L.C.C. gave us a list of possible primary schools where we might work, each satisfying the criteria we laid down, that it should be in a working-class neighbourhood, without so many immigrants as to make it quite unusual, near to the office of the Institute of Community Studies in Bethnal Green, and with a Head

The Setting for the Study

willing to co-operate. We chose John Lilburne from the list. It has been given this fictitious name in order to preserve its anonymity – this because the L.C.C. rightly insisted that 'in any published account of the research parents and pupils are not identifiable' and if we'd named the school some of them might have been. The Head has for the same reason been given the invented name of 'Mr. Pym'. Much of the comment in Chapters 2 and 3 does, by the way, refer to a period before Mr. Pym became Head.

(3) To Mr. Pym and his colleagues at John Lilburne and also to the staff at other schools where we worked.

(4) To May Clarke, Geoffrey Dench, Tamara Salaman, to other people who did interviewing, to Jean Fellows who did coding and especially to Sasha Moorsom who carried out a number of case studies of children in the remedial class.

(5) To Susannah Brown and Colin Taylor of the London School of Economics for their help with the statistics and particularly for Appendix 3, and also to Professor Alan Stuart for his initial advice.

(6) To D. N. Turland and B. Walsh for administering the tests.

(7) To the Nuffield Foundation and the Department of Education and Science who gave financial backing.

(8) To the people who commented on the draft, namely Peter Bensley, Professor Basil Bernstein, K. W. Blyth, Alan Brimer, E. H. Burden, L. J. Burrows, Sir Cyril Burt, Professor David Donnison, Euan Cooper-Willis, W. K. Elmhirst, Geoffrey Gorer, Lawrence Green, Liam Hudson, Brian Jackson, Betty Jones, Professor J. A. Lauwerys, D. J. Marshall, John Peterson, Douglas Pidgeon, Kathleen McGeeney, Harold Rose, Harry Stephenson, W. D. Wall and Peter Willmott.

(9) To the N.B.L. for arranging an exhibition.

(10) To Daphne Piccinelli who did much of the typing.

(11) Above all, to the parents, who were generous with their time; they too have been given fictitious names.

2
PARENTS' CONTACTS WITH THE SCHOOL

WE were a good deal clearer when we arrived at the school about our hopes than about how to realize them. We wanted to promote co-operation with parents. But on what? Could parents and children be persuaded to join with the students of a technical college to build their own self-help school on the bomb-site next door? We had visions of parents learning new skills and their children learning mathematics while creating a school handsome and commodious to modern eyes; and other visions of what County Hall would think. Could the school set up its own domestic radio station linked by closed circuit to every home for a daily half-hour programme? Could this be done, and that? Fantasy could reign until we had talked with the teachers and the parents. We began with the parents, asking them what their previous contacts had been with the school.

We asked all the parents in the sample what the history had been of their connection with school. The story began not with John Lilburne but at whatever Infant School their children had gone to first. Two-thirds of the mothers said they went along on the first day when their children started. The rest went with older siblings or other relatives. For nearly all the mothers the proceedings were rather perfunctory, so much so that there was very little to distinguish them from the other confrontations of working-class people with authority. When conscripted into the Services, put on to the register at 'the Labour', or when applying for a job at

Parents' Contacts with the School

the factory, it was much the same as when a child was being put to school. They had to supply 'the particulars' that bureaucracy requires.

'Not a lot happened really. They start so many children at the same time. So they just make a note of their names and addresses.'

'A lot of mothers there. Nothing about the school at all. Just taking down particulars.'

'So many start at the same time. You just take them in, hand them over to the Head of the school, and that's it.'

None of the mothers was given the opportunity to talk about the organization of the school, or about the curriculum.

The move to John Lilburne Junior School was even less of an event. Of the 40 per cent of mothers who had seen the Head then, most had children coming in from other Infant Schools.

'We took the children upstairs and the Head told us to go home.'

'It was all such a muddle. Got a note to put them in the Hall, so we left the children there. The teacher didn't want to see us.'

There was for most parents little question of choosing John Lilburne – it was just the nearest school. Only a few of them made an effort to find out about alternatives. Mr. Parr, a clerk, was one of these.

'When we got in at Jonquil House I canvassed round first to see what the local Catholic School was like, and I wasn't impressed with the lavatories there. I looked at John Lilburne, the playground and the school building, spoke to the Head and saw a couple of classes there. When I decided in favour, I tried to put the Head in the picture with regard to the qualities the children had. Told him that Janet was good at English, but, though not weak, not as good as I'd like with her sums, and that the boy was bright, very bright in fact, no doubt about that, but a little harum-scarum at times.'

Mr. Figgures, a labourer, got a book out of the local library called *How to Get a £3,000 Education on the State*. It showed

Parents' Contacts with the School

how to find out which was a good school. He inquired at the Town Hall and elsewhere, but couldn't get anything out of anyone except a list of schools and advice to 'choose' the nearest. After discussing it with relatives, he settled for John Lilburne because a cousin had a child there who seemed to be doing quite well.

Later talks with the Head

Did parents talk to Mr. Pym's predecessor on other occasions than when their children were admitted? Twenty-two per cent of the mothers, and 10 per cent of the fathers, had done so; and similar proportions had spoken to the class teacher. Few seemed to be aware they they could see the Head if they wished. A parent who had sufficient initiative and was undaunted by the NO TRESPASSING sign at the gate might eventually find herself at the top of a staircase and there discover hung on a door-knob a small printed notice telling her she was welcome to meet the Head by appointment. Few got so far. It was more common to have a word when they met by accident.

'One day I managed to curtail the Head in a corner to ask him about John.'

Some waited until there was a school medical, and seized the opportunity to seek out a member of staff then. Such special visits as were made were usually when there had been 'trouble' – for instance, when a child was away ill.

'When Richard had all his teeth out I went up to tell the teacher – just that – we didn't talk about his work.'
'If Jeremy has been at home ill from school I've gone down and asked him how he's getting on. You just knock and go in.'
'I've popped in and told him when Bertram's been queer. He told me Bertram's getting on very good.'
'I went when Billy had some trouble with nose bleeding. It was to stop "the Visitor" coming.'

This last father, an Irishman, gave the impression that for

Parents' Contacts with the School

him 'the Visitor' (or School Attendance Officer) was a fearsome figure. In Eire he was apparently quick to bring parents into court. Another mother was mystified by the 'charisma' of the Head.

'I went up to the school to see the teacher because Barney had to stay at home with those dizzy spells. This was owing to have to stare at the Head during Assembly. The Head told him, "You mustn't take your eyes off me." I said I'm sure you could lower them *sometimes*. But he won't; he just stared. That was a bit scary for him, wasn't it?'

Then there were the children who got into fights – nearly always, as the parents saw it, at the instigation of some other 'hooligan', not of their own child. They either sought out the Head or were called by him.

'One or two of them were getting John up against the wall and punching him. I had to go up to see about that. Afterwards I caught one of them in the road myself and says to him, "Come on, what is it, a punch across the ear-hole from me or the nearest police station?" You can guess what the lad chose.'

'Some boys knocked him in the playground and broke Graham's arm. They were just playing, I think, but I went up.'

'The only time I saw her was when I went up to complain about some boys. One boy took Geraldine's pen in class and said if she wanted it back she'd have to strip. On the way home the boy had a friend with him who tried to get hold of her. She was so scared she couldn't even eat her tea. I think they ought to have had the cane for that.'

Just occasionally the parents didn't try to pin blame on anyone else. They knew it was no use. When the interviewer arrived at Mr. Harper's, for instance, his arm was gripped in alarm. 'I know, don't tell me, it's Barry, isn't it? What's he been up to this time? He's a little terror, that lad.' Mr. Harper had been to see the Head when one of the masters beat Barry.

'When he came home from school the marks were still on him. He was sore all night. Next morning the marks were still there.

Parents' Contacts with the School

The master said he didn't cane him hard enough and nearly fetched him back for another because he didn't cry. The Head was very nice about it.'

Mr. Harper had bought Barry a fruit machine – a one-armed bandit – so that the two of them could try for jackpots at home. It was the one present Barry had set his heart on. Mrs. Harper thought Barry must be alright at bottom because 'I think all people who like animals are good people. So he must be good, mustn't he?' His father did not mind him fighting as long as he joined in with other English to fight 'the Catholics'. The battle of 'English versus Catholics' was something all self-respecting children should take part in.

Other teachers

The Head apparently used to believe that parents who were worried about their children should see him rather than their class teacher. If he sought a monopoly, it was not for selfish reasons. His motive was to protect the staff against the parents. He saw himself, with some justice, as the pivot of the school – the figure who was relatively permanent, unlike so many of the transitory teachers; even if they did not move on elsewhere, they would keep a child for only one year. His tenure meant he could build up a relationship with parents which might last all the time their children were at the school. He wanted to be the first to know, even if only from a hint, whether anything had happened which might cause a public row, of the kind that might come to the attention of the Local Education Authority, an ever watchful presence in the background. He considered he should always be available in an emergency.

Parents still knew a good deal at second hand through their children about the class teachers even though, like Mrs. Verona, 'I've never actually spoken to Jill's teacher – but I saw him once.' Nearly half the parents knew the name of their child's teacher, and usually had some stereotype to

Parents' contacts with the School

go with the name – he's the strict one, she does the swimming, he's from India, she's kind with them, and so forth. Occasionally, too, they met and talked when they went into the school (the teacher whose classroom was by the main entrance was seen much more than other teachers), or if they had the temerity to knock on the classroom door or the foresight to be in the right place to catch the teacher as she was rushing away after school hours for her car and for home. One mother was so agitated by the odd circumstance that her son wrote his name backwards that she waylaid his teacher, who reassured her (again oddly) by saying, 'It must be the way he sees the lesson.' Another thought it wrong that her son who was notably backward should also be at the back of the class, at the back with all the other backward children, and asked the teacher several times, though without success, to shift him to the front. Yet another went up to ask Mr. Hazlitt, one of the teachers, to move a daughter whose continuing earache she attributed to the draught by the door. This time Mr. Hazlitt responded and put another child in the draught instead. When Brian Murphy came home vomiting, Mrs. Murphy saw his teacher, who said he might have rushed his dinner to make himself sick and get home early. Mrs. Churchill was angered by the paint her son spilt on his shorts, and brought the trousers up for the teacher to see. 'Couldn't he wear a bib when he paints?' Another teacher actually sent for a mother to tell her that her daughter cried too much when spoken to sharply.

Open Day

These were informal contacts. The great formal occasion of the year was Open Day, in the summer term. In the year before the interview, 65 per cent of the mothers and 43 per cent of the fathers came to it.

For weeks the preparations had been going on; at last the exhibits from each class were ready for display in the Assembly Hall, each showing something of the wide variety

Parents' Contacts with the School

of work that had been done during the year. One class had concentrated on Nature. Rows of butterflies were pinned on sheets of cartridge paper. Another had built a large papier mâché Noah's Ark. There was a collection of glove puppets and of bark rubbings and a contour map of the Forest of Arden where the fourth-year children had been for the annual outing. Lines of open notebooks were pinned to the wall. 'One day my father ran into some cash at the betting office' was the start of one story. Another sheet was dappled with ducks, to illustrate the verse set in its middle:

DUCK'S DITTY

(From 'The Wind in the Willows')

> All along the backwater,
> Through the rushes tall,
> Ducks are a-dabbling,
> Up tails all!

The parents began to arrive in a rush, soon after 3.0 p.m. Some of them had never been in the school before. Older children were waiting at the top of the gangway to tell them which classroom to go to. Once there, the parents queued up if (as for most of the time in the day) the room was crowded, for a word with the strict one, the swimming lady, or whoever it might be. The teacher handed over a written report on the child, answered the usual question, 'How's he getting on?', and said that the mother or father was welcome to look at their child's work. The parents, nudged a bit from behind, passed to the books. For a few minutes they wedged themselves into a child's desk and went through the ritual; even if they had not been before, they seemed to know what was expected of them. They thumbed through the exercise books. As soon as this was over the child was called out to lead the way to the Assembly Hall, or, if the parent had another child in the school, to another classroom to repeat the procedure.

Parents' Contacts with the School

On the way to the Hall parents passed the library, where another little ceremony was in progress. Some of the Managers were having tea and biscuits and light conversation with the Head. On the right was the Vicar in his high white collar, on the left a wiry shrewd-faced member of the Local Council, opposite two unplaced elderly ladies of undefeated gentility. The door was open so that the tea-drinkers could look out at the shuffling parents, for whom there was no tea, and the parents could look in on the gentry.

This was as we saw it. How did it look to the parents? We asked the sample. Most were satisfied. It had all come up to their expectations. Some were really delighted by the work and by this first chance to see the teacher their child had had for nearly a year. 'I have no suggestions for improvement. We found the lady teacher very willing.' 'I enjoyed it. I didn't even know my little girl had done such good sewing.' But even many of the generally satisfied ones were critical of the crush and the queue in the classroom. 'There's such a long waiting period when all parents come at once. Couldn't we be given set times to come for the interview, or be alphabetically spread over two or three days?' Another complaint was about the lack of privacy in the classroom:

> 'One big thing we're against is showing up one child. You're sitting there on Open Day talking to the teacher and she says "Now look at that work there (picking up an exercise book of one of Pauline's classmates), look how much better and neater it is", and Pauline and their child are standing there listening to it. It's not right.'
>
> 'Doug wasn't getting on too well. I knew they sometimes put them in the backward class. The teacher turned to me and asked me right there with all the others whether they "ought to put you down with the dim ones", didn't she, Doug?'

Others did not say they minded so much about the lack of privacy, which perhaps they'd got used to, as about the 'report' they got at this crucial encounter.

Parents' Contacts with the School

'I was disappointed in Amanda. Maybe I thought she was going to be clever, and the teacher said she isn't. I had hoped she'd go to a grammar school like me – but I don't think she will at this rate.'
'Open Days? Well, I go off hoping for the best but expecting the worst. As you might say, more or less with an open mind. Some things I find I'm rather pleased about. You ask the teacher for the classroom and she says "Janet sits over there". You look at their work and they ask if you have any questions. I think her objection was that Janet chattered far too much.'

The other main formal occasion of the year was a play, in the Easter term. All the parents were enthusiastic about it, without demur. The Head wrote and produced it himself, and managed to get very large numbers of children into it. 'They're really marvellous. Last time Griselda was standing right by me. I didn't recognize her, the way she was dressed. It was ever so clever.' 'It was just like a West End production, with all the lighting.'

There was also a meeting during the year for all parents to explain the new arrangements for secondary school selection which were introduced at that time. The ones who came seemed neither for nor against, merely puzzled about the difference the change would in practice make for their children. At the end of the formal meeting the Head said that discussion could continue on other topics, and 25 of the most articulate and critical parents stayed on. They made several suggestions. The Public Baths were too far away for young children to be transported there regularly. The parents wanted their own school swimming pool, and seemed ready to build it. They thought that one day in the year was not enough of an opportunity to find out all they wanted to know from their class teacher about their child's progress. They wanted to form a Parent-Teacher Association. They wanted a crossing-man paid by the parents so that it would be less dangerous to get over the main road outside the school. They wanted to replace 'those shocking lavatories'. When the swishing of cleaners' brushes from the

Parents' Contacts with the School

wings became too loud the meeting was closed; the 25 bottled their eagerness and went quietly home.

This then is a brief account, seen through the eyes of the parents alone, of their contacts with the school before any changes were made. Many of them came to and appreciated the Open Day and the school play. Criticisms came from only a minority, and especially from the 25 who when an opportunity was presented stayed behind after the formal meeting to fire suggestions at the Head. These annual occasions apart, they rarely saw Head or teachers, except when there was 'trouble' of one sort or another. Comparison with the Plowden Report suggests that in its annual round John Lilburne was not so unlike the rest of the primary schools in the country. Something like this may be the situation in many places.

3
PARENTS' ATTITUDES BEFORE THE TRIAL

THE last chapter discussed contacts with the school. We needed to know the existing situation before we tried to change it. After that, we had to gauge parents' attitudes. Was there a sufficient fund of goodwill towards the school and interest in it to justify the hope that, if teachers invited the parents, at any rate some of them would come? If not, the trial would hardly be worthwhile making. The next question was whether the parents were critical enough of some features of the school to want some changes. This is not a contradiction. If the parents had not thought well of the school they might have spurned any approach; but, at the opposite extreme, they might have thought so well of it that they did not see any point in changing anything. These anyway are the two initial questions discussed in this chapter. At the end there is a third – about the influence of parental encouragement on children's performance. We could not assume that the two would be linked at John Lilburne. We had to find out. If they had not been, there would again have been no purpose in launching the trial. There would have been no reason to expect that any heightening of parental encouragement at the instance of the school would raise the children's performance.

The first question is fairly easy to answer. Fifty-nine per cent of the parents said they felt the education their children were getting at John Lilburne was as good as that of most children of the same age in Britain, 10 per cent said better, 7 per cent worse and the rest were not sure. The

Parents' Attitudes before the Trial

commendation by the parents was usually based on a comparison they made over time. Ninety-five per cent of the parents thought that their children had a better chance than when they were at school. Particularly noteworthy was the change in relations between teachers and children.

'When I was at school I was terrified to ask the teacher anything if once she'd explained it, but they don't seem like that today. If they don't understand, they'll put their hands up and tell her they don't. There's a lot better feeling between teacher and child.'

'We were always frightened to speak to our teachers. Today the children are more free and easy with them.'

'We laughed – John corrected the teacher the other day, told him he'd spelled bicycle wrong on the board, and the teacher said so he had.

'My mum says the children seem to be born with more brains today. Television is a big help. And the teachers are much younger than the ones we had – old ladies who were behind the times. The teachers dress more modern and talk to them in their own language. For instance, John's teacher speak about the Beatles, and talks to him about his baby brother.'

Children were less frightened than they used to be. They were handled more sympathetically, especially by Mr. Pym, the Head.

'We had a lot of trouble with Ronnie. Very nervous child – he used to think I was going to run away. I took him back the first morning he ran home. And we sat down and had a little talk with Mr. Pym and he took Ronnie back into his class. Mr. Pym dealt with it marvellously. He said to Ronnie, "Come to me any time you get a funny feeling". He gave him a job dishing out cakes. That made Ronnie feel important. A very generous man is Mr. Pym.'

This friendliness of teachers was all the more remarkable because they were so badly paid (as the parents saw it), and so hard pressed. 'They ought to be awarded the George Medal, every one of them! It would drive me barmy taking 35 to 40 kids all day long.'

Parents' Attitudes before the Trial

The sharpest contrasts of all were made by people from overseas. Some of them emigrated partly for the sake of the good schools that were known to exist in England. Mr. Fiorello said that in England, unlike Italy, 'education depends on merit, not money'. Some parents from Ireland were quite as enthusiastic. There, according to Mr. Halloran, it used to be all 'teaching by the strap' when he had been a child.

> 'There were 60 in a class – all in one room. The teachers used to take you out if you were even five minutes late in the morning and hammer you up against the blackboard until the blood began to run. Some boys had their noses broken with the thumps the teacher gave them. We used to go to school in bare feet. Now in England Tim will go to a new school when he's eleven and he'll even have his own inkwell.'

Such happy contrasts did not, of course, necessarily make parents visit the school. Some of them, whether Irish or English, who had been at schools they would rather forget, seemed to be so satisfied with John Lilburne that they did not feel they had to show any interest in it. Their children were in such eminently good hands. Mr. Moody, who said

> 'When I was at school what I learned you could have put on a postage stamp'

was so pleased with all his son was learning that he had never been up to the school at all.

Interest in education

They had goodwill towards the school partly because they had goodwill towards education. Most of the parents were over 35 and had, therefore, left school at 14 or under before the 1944 Act came into force. Many had been evacuated.

> 'I was nine, a very critical age, when the war broke out. You were just pushed into a Church Hall and had to knit for the soldiers. I cried so much I had to come home.'

Parents' Attitudes before the Trial

Whether in this predicament or not, most parents would have liked more education than they obtained. Regret about leaving school so early was common. Mr. Benson wanted to take up science but had to leave and get a job to help his mother. 'Our family,' he said, 'was glad to get that job.' Mr. Smith's efforts to carry on his education came to nothing. When forced to leave school against his will he chose to work as a lab boy in a Technical College so that he could watch the experiments and learn some physics and chemistry. He regretted that he had to give that up too for more money in an office for the sake of his many younger brothers and sisters. He and his wife, who had been a shorthand typist, had so many books in the house that 'you could open a library with them'. Here, surely, was one man who would come to the school if the teachers asked him?

Most parents hoped their children would have more education than they had themselves. The commonest reason was that education is now essential for a good job. One man, more or less illiterate, said that 'Reading would have have been a great asset to me'; another that, 'A well-writ letter is as good as a good job. It doesn't matter what you're like afterwards as long as you can write them a good letter when you are after a job. Now, however good a worker I am, I can't get more than a certain amount of money.' Aspirations for children extended even to girls.

> 'I hope she'll stay at school longer than I did. I think she should get good qualifications. It's important, you know. People say "Oh, she's only a girl." But I think, well, even suppose she does marry, a husband can die. She ought to be able to keep herself.'

The bulk of parents who would have liked more education for themselves had not ordinarily done anything about it. Mr. Knight was one of the few who had. A machine operator in an engineering factory, he was a keen trade unionist. When he went to meetings he found that when he got up to speak the words came out wrong: he could not say what he meant to.

Parents' Attitudes before the Trial

'So me and my mates went to a public speaking class at the Evening Institute. At first we all sat there in the class. Not a word out of any of us. When he asked me to speak, my mind just went blank. But by the end of the term he had us on our feet out in front. It did me a world of good, that course did. They were amazed at the union meetings at the change. They can't make it out. We've sprung it on them. You enjoy it when you know you have got something to say and that the others take notice of you – you know, when you can move them to your way of thinking.'

The criticisms

The parents were interested. Were they also critical? Many parents, as we have seen, praised the teachers for being so friendly; others thought them much too friendly. Mr. Watson said:

'When I was at school and did wrong I was biffed on the backside. And when I got home at night my father did it all over again. It's all altered now. I don't think the youngsters of today are any better off because of it.'

Mrs. Cooksley likewise:

'I myself don't think they're strict enough. Schools have altered a lot even since the two eldest here went to school. Nowadays they take it all as one happy jungle. Youngsters don't seem like children these days. Instead of the children being ruled by the teachers, the teachers seem to be ruled by them.'

People like Mr. Watson and Mrs. Cooksley thought that by far the best teachers were the ones who hit the children and had a reputation for being disciplinarians.

Several of the parents who thought the teachers were not strict enough mysteriously seemed to feel unable to impose the necessary degree of discipline at home. Critical of teachers for being like, instead of unlike, themselves, they sometimes even appeared to bask in their helplessness. The Berelson children, for instance, jumped up from bed when the interviewer arrived, and, despite all remonstrance,

Parents' Attitudes before the Trial

refused to budge from the room. An hour later mother and father tried again. The two boys again refused and one of them tweaked his father's nose, which made the whole family laugh with great satisfaction.

Allied with this complaint was another, about the undue prominence of 'play'.

> 'The curriculum is to be thought of in terms of activity and experience rather than of knowledge to be acquired and facts to be stored.'

This, the Hadow doctrine of 1931, has not yet been accepted by some of these parents. A few thought their children had too much play. In the Infants School they merely messed about, a great disappointment to some of the children who had been told by parents that as soon as they had achieved the dignity of going to school they would begin to 'learn'. In the Junior School they had too much of 'just singing' – 'It drove you up the sausage, didn't it, Milly?' – instead of getting on with the serious purposes for which schools exist. Instead of the playing about and the singing the children should learn foreign languages and have homework. 'Homework lets the parents get more of an insight into what the children are doing at school, and they can get the pulse of how the child is getting on.' The criticism of Hadow did not on the whole extend to arts and crafts. Most parents could see what their children had achieved, and appreciate it. One father was so enthusiastic about the paintings he saw on Open Day that he took a batch of colour photographs of them for his collection. One mother could almost have been herself quoting from Hadow or Plowden.

> 'They are allowed to draw what they like now. Their imagination can come out. It's a good thing. There's more freedom. They are not told *what* to do. It's more interesting for them that way.'

Many parents were firmly critical of the 'shocking' lavatories, of the lack of playing fields, or of the dress for PT –

Parents' Attitudes before the Trial

'In winter-time horsing about in vests and pants and catching cold; it's not right' – and the arrangements for swimming.

> 'Jock went one Tuesday and he came back and said someone'd ducked him. He got frightened about it. He used to get terribly sick from his stomach on Friday night even before the Tuesday. I had to go and see Mr. Pym about that.'

What was striking about the interviews was that the parents were for the most part so much firmer in their comments about discipline and lavatories and swimming than they were about the methods of teaching used, that is apart from the general comment on play. About teaching methods they were confused. They were ignorant, they knew they were ignorant, and they were therefore a little fearful.

All many of them knew was that teaching methods were different from when they were at school – more so in some parts of the curriculum than others, as the following table shows.

TABLE I
PARENTS' AWARENESS OF DIFFERENCE IN TEACHING METHODS

	Reading	Arithmetic	Physical Education	Arts & Crafts
Much the same	31%	24%	39%	39%
Different	46%	57%	37%	34%
Don't know	23%	19%	24%	27%
TOTAL %	100%	100%	100%	100%
No.	117	118	118	116

Methods of reading

Whether or not they thought there had been a change in method, those who refused to 'interfere' (as some put it) with school work were in a small minority. Few had been able to avoid getting involved in their children's efforts to

Parents' Attitudes before the Trial

learn. Many of the children came home and tried to repeat what they had been doing in school. When they appealed for help, it was often in vain. Take reading as an example. Many parents had themselves started at school by learning the alphabet, and could see that this was no longer in vogue.

> 'They don't learn them the alphabet, which I thought would have been better. They learn them more by looking at pictures. We had to teach the boy the alphabet ourselves.'
> 'I think they have Look and Learn, which is different to what we had.'
> 'When I try to help him he says we don't do it that way. They have to learn words in a block – you know, bits of words. Then they also learn words in a piece all at once.'
> 'When I've tried to teach her reading it's different. Their reading is in sorts of pairs of words. They seem to read it more like poetry.'
> 'The teacher tells the children to speak the word and write it down all at once. I think that's very advanced.'

Quite a number of parents, like the first one quoted above, decided that the children were not getting on well enough and must know their ABC, proceeded to teach them, and then tried to build up the words from there. 'I tried the cat-on-the-mat stuff time and time again. I tried to stuff it into them but it didn't work. It wouldn't go in.' In families with several children it was sometimes the older children, more abreast with modern ideas, who did the teaching rather than the parents. 'The two older daughters have already taught the youngster to count, and they're teaching her to read now.' In others it was grandparents, remembering even earlier schooldays, who took a hand.

Once the child had begun to grasp how to do it, it was easier for the parents.

> 'I listen to him read if he wants to. Never push him. If he says listen to me read, I do.'
> 'He's a good little reader. A lovely little reader is Tommy. He pronounces the big words perfectly. That's a thing he is good at.'

Parents' Attitudes before the Trial

At a later stage still, when the child could read easily on his own, many of the parents seemed to feel their job was over. There was no need for them to do anything more.

'Not unless it's something she can't understand. Otherwise she gets annoyed if you talk to her when she's reading. She's too old to be read to now. She would laugh her head off if I offered.'

Not many parents recognized the continuing importance of books. Nearly one-third of them said their children were members of the public library. Of the rest, some knew where the nearest branch was but considered it too far for their children to walk to, across many busy roads. Others did not know where it was, how to join, when it was open, or for what ages it catered. 'I don't know if they'll let Veronica have books. She's only eight.' Others, again, feared that books would not be taken back in time and a fine levied. There was almost as much ignorance about the school library – a lot of parents did not know whether children were allowed to bring books home from it or not.

The parents were, it seemed, in need of guidance about libraries, and also about the sort of books to buy. Eighty-four per cent said that someone – often a grandparent, other relative or friend – had bought at least one book for their child in the previous twelve months. But the choice was somewhat indiscriminating. Annuals were the most popular. 'Books' were sometimes interpreted to mean comics – 'Yes, I buy him fairy stories and comics.' Then there were encyclopaedias. For some parents these were a kind of magic. The belief seemed to be that merely by possessing all these large volumes, their children would, by a form of osmosis, without actually opening the covers, absorb the knowledge they contained. For this talisman it was worth handing over to the salesman instalments totalling up to £40 or even, for one set, as much as £80.

Parents' Attitudes before the Trial

Arithmetic

It was much the same with arithmetic. Even the tiniest differences in methods since the parents were at school could be a source of confusion.

> 'Well, arithmetic is different today. If you want to add, say, 115 and 56, we would carry one. But they put it underneath.'
> 'The way they do arithmetic! They even do tables differently. Whereas we said 1 times 2 = 2, 2 times 2 = 4, they teach them 2 times 1 = 2, 2 times 2 = 4, and so on.'
> 'They work differently now. They get the same answers but now you do it backwards – the multiplying that is.'

The attempt to give children realistic problems to work out was not necessarily appreciated either. Here are Mr. and Mrs. Gudgeon.

> *Mr. Gudgeon:* 'They've just given my eldest girl a problem to work out. Sounds potty to me. That is, if she's got the facts right. She may have got it wrong.'
> *Mrs. Gudgeon:* 'They've been asked to work out a three-course meal for two people at home. To spend £1 exactly. Well, I've worked out a marvellous meal with the most expensive things we can think of and I can't get it to more than 13/10d.'
> *Mr. Gudgeon:* 'On that basis, I've worked out I should have to give my wife £27 a week housekeeping. Imagine it! And we spend our time trying to teach the children to economize!!'

Yet many parents did try to help. To assist with reading was more often the woman's duty in so far as it was anyone's, 'sums' or 'figurework' the man's. Others gave up when they saw they were only muddling the child. 'We showed him how and the teacher marked them wrong, and it wasn't the answers that were wrong but the way of working out. So I said in future you must go the way of the teacher, not me.' 'The teachers have got their set ways, so you don't like to poke your nose in.'

There was also a good deal of ignorance about the general organization of the school. Many parents did not understand,

Parents' Attitudes before the Trial

for instance, the principles on which children were brought together in forms, and especially about streaming. John Lilburne was in the final stages of unstreaming, only the fourth year still being streamed. The parents were in a muddle about it. Some were sure the school did have streaming throughout, though 'hushed up so the children don't know about it'. One parent regretted it because the selection of children for one or other stream was so arbitrary, but not so much as in a neighbouring school where it was alleged to be worse. 'They put children in classes according to their height. I think that's wrong. They jump up children three or four classes just because of their height.' Others regretted it because streaming meant that 'they only look after the bright ones and let the other ones fall behind. You go up on Open Day and there's the same half-dozen children around the teachers all the time. The others just plod along'. On the other hand, there were a few parents with bright children who, by another twist, thought the school did not have streaming and that it was hard on their own children.

> 'When I was at school they separated us and never let us keep with other children who was slower, so I got a scholarship to the Technical School. Bright children should not get stuck with the common herd, as they are at John Lilburne.'

The school was only at the end of the street. But to judge by the way they talked about it, for many parents it could almost have been in another world. They could see the massive walls; they did not understand what went on behind them. They did not understand because they had never been told, except by their children, who were not always the best of informants. Nearly all the parents frequently asked them how they were getting on. They usually got vague answers. 'You can never get much sense out of Tony about what he's done right or wrong at school.' 'I asked Brenda but she doesn't give me a definite answer.' One Italian mother was very insistent.

Parents' Attitudes before the Trial

'I ask every day, is he all right. Every day he say "Everything fine", but we don't know if something missing. And my husband, believe me, he even ask more. "What do you learn? Do you learn enough?" Sometimes I talk to my husband and he say, "Go to school and ask how he do." I would like to speak to teacher, but don't like to disturb. I want to know right thing what Mario do. Don't know what he say right or wrong. You like to know *properly*.'

A few were reconciled to their ignorance. They had tried to understand and failed. 'There's lots I'd like to talk to the kids about but in a way we don't speak the same language. When Jackie was in Mr. Barlow's class, and was having bother with maths, I asked Mr. Barlow if I could help in any way but when he pointed things out to me I couldn't because I didn't understand it myself.' Some were quite simply glad that it was someone else's business to worry about their children when they were out of the home. But some were chafing. They wanted to talk to the child's teacher, see inside the school and begin to find out how it worked. Mrs. Robinson, though more articulate than most, spoke for several when she said:

'I'd just like to know how they do teach today, compared to what they did when I was at school. I know there was a war on when I was at school. I'd like to be able to make it a bit easier for the teachers. They must have a lot on with a class. They can't give individual help all the time. If a child doesn't understand a subject, the teacher could say, "Take it home tonight. Show it to Mummy and Daddy." We could help if we knew how to.'

It was on the Mrs. Robinsons that we should evidently have to rely in the months to follow.

Measures of encouragement

We come, finally, to our third question, about the effect of encouragement by parents. We have just been saying that most of them were unsure about what to do for the best. But

Parents' Attitudes before the Trial

there were still noticeable differences between parents. Some were not put off by their ignorance of modern mathematics; they still played games with their children like Monopoly 'which is helpful from the counting angle – it's a cunning sort of motive to get them to learn'. Some took them on outings to see the sights of London, or involved them in their own hobbies, or read to them regularly. Others did not.

The questions asked in order to assess the extent of parental encouragement were not nearly as pointed as we would have liked. As yet, no one knows in a systematic way what it is about a home which creates a favourable or an unfavourable atmosphere for learning. Nor about a school, for that matter. Some teachers evidently have a gift with some children, others do not; some combinations of teachers supplement instead of frustrating each other. Likewise with mothers and fathers, and with combinations of people in the immediate and extended families which children join at birth.

What is the gift that some parents have? Their love and respect for their children? We could in our interviews perhaps sense that some had more than others; we could not with our crude questionnaires come to grips with such fundamentals. Their intelligence? We could have tried to measure that, but dared not for fear of making ourselves as unwelcome as any 'visitor'. We were going to visit each family twice anyway for fairly long spells within the space of six months, and the parents were going to have other taxing demands laid upon them by the school. Was it their ability to use the environment of the home for educational purposes? This is not necessarily the same thing as intelligence. The Hadow doctrine mentioned a few moments ago is certainly as applicable to the home as to the school, and may well be more so. Learning by 'activity and experience' goes on in it every day from morning to night. How effectively must depend on the power of the parents to discriminate colour and texture, sounds and shapes, and on the

Parents' Attitudes before the Trial

sensitivity of the language they use to express what they think and feel. From the earliest days of 'one, two, three, four, five – Once I caught a fish alive' to the discussion of a Western on the television, language is used, with greater or lesser effect, to differentiate and at the same time bring order into the child's universe, which to begin with means his home. Whether the parents are themselves interested, not just in the child, but in all that is around him and them may more than anything else effect the child's ability to relate himself to his external world, and his motivation to try.

We know that the questions we asked to gauge the educational atmosphere of the home were fumbling, and in the existing state of knowledge, perhaps had to be. Case studies have not yet been made on any scale of children as they develop over all their earliest years in the course of interaction with the shifting but patterned constellations of people who form their environment. Until that is done we shall not even have workmanlike hypotheses about the effects of many different styles of upbringing, and we shall certainly not begin to understand what may be called 'the Chekhov mystery'.[1] Exceptional children, like Anton Chekhov himself, become men of genius despite (or because of?) having suffered the most abysmally miserable childhoods; others with no apparent suffering and even every positive advantage lapse into a jaded apathy.

As it is, we do not know what are the things about the home that matter, and, since we do not know, we obviously cannot be sure that the questions we asked are even within their limits the most pertinent ones. All we could do was to ask questions that lent themselves to fairly definite answers and which even so seemed worth asking. We knew we might easily miss the truth. We asked, for instance, whether parents bought books for their children, and found this was related to progress at school. This does not necessarily mean that

---

[1] Magarshack, D., *Chekhov the Dramatist*, also Illingworth & Illingworth, *Lessons from Childhood*.

Parents' Attitudes before the Trial

buying books actually does matter (although we would think that it probably does). The purchase of books may just happen to go with an attitude to literacy and learning, and the attitude may matter so much more than any particular expression of it in behaviour, that a parent with the attitude would do well by her children whether or not she ever went near a bookshop.

The questions we put are in the questionnaire printed as Appendix 2. In practice we assessed the extent of parental interest in two main ways. We did it by reference to behaviour within the home – apart from that question about books, we asked whether parents read to them in the evenings, whether they helped with school-work, whether they played with them, whether they talked to the child about how they were getting on at school, and (since we took it that parents would usually determine the issue) whether the children belonged to the public library and borrowed books from the school. We also did it by reference to the contacts actually made with the school, and the knowledge about it – whether the parents attended the Open Day, or School Shows, or had talked to the Head and to teachers, and whether they knew which class the child was in and whether it was a streamed or an unstreamed one. We also attempted to measure their children's 'performance' at school, and for this purpose used the four tests, of Verbal Intelligence, Non-Verbal Intelligence, Reading and Arithmetic, described in Appendix 1. As a first approach to relating the degree of parental encouragement to educational performance we summarized the former by giving a score to parents according to their answers to the questions we asked, and the latter by the scores of their children on the tests. In Table 2 the parents have been divided as far as they could be into four more or less equal groups. The Table reveals a marked association between parental interest, as summarized in this way, and educational performance.

Parents' Attitudes before the Trial

TABLE 2
RELATION BETWEEN SCORES FOR PARENTAL ENCOURAGEMENT AND FOR EDUCATIONAL PERFORMANCE OF CHILDREN

Encouragement Score Groups	Verbal No.	Score	Non-verbal No.	Score	Reading No.	Score	Arithmetic No.	Score
Top Group	21	111·09	21	113·95	21	103·24	21	99·86
2nd Group	29	99·00	31	102·52	30	96·53	31	93·55
3rd Group	32	96·78	32	97·97	32	92·37	30	92·67
Bottom Group	32	88·37	32	97·94	32	86·91	31	88·61
Level of Statistical Significance of the Regression of Performance Scores on Scores for Encouragement		0·1%		0·1%		0·1%		1%

Table 2 does not give any indication of the relative importance of the different kinds of encouragement or of other relevant features of the environment – such as the occupation of the father. It was of obvious interest to try and find out. For this purpose we used a regression analysis similar to that designed by Gilbert Peaker and described in the Plowden Report. A regression analysis is a way of measuring the interactions of a large number of factors rather than considering each factor on its own. Simple correlations for the associations, say, between children's scores on the reading tests and the mothers' practice of playing, or not playing, with them are liable to be misleading. The correlation would lie (as with all correlations) between +1 and −1. The simple correlation in this case was +0·266. But a comparison of such simple correlations for the association of different

Parents' Attitude before the Trial

variables with performance might be misleading, because the variables being related to performance might all be correlated with each other. To assess the importance of this practice on the part of mothers it was necessary to calculate what it was correlated with – age, for instance. It turned out that more older mothers played with their children than younger ones, and that the children of older mothers had higher scores. Thus, when age was held constant, and mothers of similar age who did or did not play with their children were compared, the correlations with performance were reduced, although only by a little. Taking account of age meant that this particular practice was seen as less important. The regression analysis shows by means of a regression coefficient how each variable is related to performance after the bearing of all other variables has been taken into account.

The factors we have already mentioned as figuring in the scores for parental encouragement were included in the analysis, and many others as well, as explained in Appendix 3. We also included other groups of variables which we thought of for convenience as relating to 'family background' rather than 'parental encouragement' – the occupation of the father, for example, family size, the mother's and father's age and the length of education of the parents. We did this so that we could estimate the relative importance of these variables as against different forms of parental interest. The results are reproduced in the tables in Appendix 3.

There are three main conclusions which can be drawn from the run of tables in that Appendix.

(1) In general, they support the Plowden findings. Parental encouragement clearly mattered a very great deal to the children at John Lilburne as it does generally. This finding has already been discussed in the Plowden Report. It is a hopeful one. For it would not have come out like this unless many working-class parents do in fact give effective encouragement to their children. What many working-class people already do, perhaps others will do tomorrow; and it

Parents' Attitude before the Trial

may be possible to speed up the process of change by action initiated from the school.

(2) The tables also show which variables are most closely linked with performance. Membership of the library is more so than anything else. This hint about the continuing importance of books in an age of television is certainly not without interest. Whether the mother plays with her child or not also appears to matter a good deal.

(3) From a series of negative correlations in the tables, it appears that fathers read to their children more, and play more with them, when they are *not* doing well at school. Likewise for mothers reading to them. Fathers had also spoken more often to the Head or a class teacher where their child's performance was low. It was always obvious that some parents would encourage their children more fully if they were already doing well. We now see that the opposite also happens, and once the fact is pointed out it becomes easy to accept. It is perfectly plausible that fathers should take more trouble to read to a child or play with one who is, as one father put it, 'choking on the long words', or go up in a worried state to see the Head or a teacher when a child is doing particularly badly at school. There were also included in our sample a few parents who seemed to be 'encouraging' their children so much that they were holding them back, infecting the young with the anxiety of the old. The relationship between parental interest and performance is evidently more complicated than we thought.

Now to sum up – the preliminary inquiries mentioned in this chapter gave us heart to proceed. Although we could do no more than gather impressions about the parents' attitudes, for what it was worth the view we formed in the course of our talks with the parents in their homes was that they were by and large interested in their children's education and at the same time sufficiently critical of some features of this particular school to justify a more vigorous attempt to win their co-operation. The analysis of the relationship between performance and parental encouragement was also hopeful.

Parents' Attitude before the Trial

The children of parents who took an interest in their education did on the whole (though not always as we have seen) do better at school than others. If more of the parents could be persuaded to take more interest, the general level of performance might be raised. It seemed worth trying to find out what could be done.

4
THE CHANGES IN THE SCHOOL

FROM what they said it seemed that the parents were interested and would be willing for closer co-operation. They also gave their opinion about the value of the various suggestions we put to them, and volunteered some of their own. After the survey our view was that four proposals in particular would be worth discussing further – an open meeting early in the term for all parents, or as many of them as would come; private talks between individual parents and the class teachers'; meetings on teaching methods – this because of the worry we have reported about innovations since the parents were at school; and home visits for some of the parents who would not come to the school. What happened under these four heads will be described in a moment. What was done for immigrants is considered in the next chapter.

We did not, of course, take the answers parents gave to our questions at their face value. Ninety-six per cent of the informants said they would willingly go up for a talk with the class teacher – we did not believe it. Nor the 97 per cent who said they would attend meetings on teaching methods. We doubted partly because our questions were in general terms – no specific times were, or at that stage could be, given for any new ventures at the school. We knew that whatever time was chosen would automatically rule out many people who might otherwise come. One out of three fathers worked irregular hours, including night shifts, and if they weren't at home at night the mothers often couldn't get out either. Baby-sitting was a problem for almost all the

The Changes in the School

parents. Many mothers would not go out at night by themselves and yet couldn't go with their husbands because the children would then be left alone. Of the men with regular hours nearly a fifth were not back home till after 7 p.m., which didn't make it easy to have tea and leave again for an evening meeting, that is, even if they weren't too tired for it after a long day's work. An added complication (as we have mentioned in Chapter 1) was that over half of the mothers were out at work themselves. Many parents spontaneously cautioned us about this, and proposed Saturday instead of evening meetings. They had not reckoned on the teachers. Now that church attendance is less than it was, the new day of rest on Saturday is almost as sacrosanct as Sunday. One way of making things easier for parents though not for teachers is to repeat all meetings and occasions just as though they were star television programmes. To hold a second meeting would be better a week, rather than a day, later, as fathers are more likely to change shifts weekly than daily; and at least one of the Open Days should be an Open Night. If only one time is possible, there are bound to be many parents who will just not be able to come.

This caution apart, the parents seemed willing for something. How about the teachers? Would they be also? We knew we had to choose a school where at any rate the Head would be ready for change. We were lucky in Mr. Pym. Like all other Heads we had seen he said he had 'good relations with parents'.[1] We did not set too much store by that. But he was a parent himself, coping with other teachers on behalf of a child of his at another primary school, and that meant he was more likely, from his other role, to sympathize with the point of view of parents. He was new to John Lilburne and was therefore not too set in his ways. In many schools change comes at its fastest in the early years of a new Headship. He also thought that the need to explain things to

[1] See Wall, W.D., 'The opinions of Teachers on Parent-Teacher co-operation' —a pioneer study in this field.

The Changes in the School

parents might be a lever for getting an improvement in the quality of teaching.

Mr. Pym's co-operation was one thing, that of the staff another. Apart from Mr. Pym, they numbered 15 full-time and two part-time. Three of the full-time teachers left during the trial: one went sick, one went abroad and one into a maternity ward. Naturally, no teacher said he opposed closer co-operation with parents – that is the sort of platitude which commands agreement precisely because it means almost nothing. Yet, after mild agreement on such a generality, disquiet soon began to be expressed. Why should they be pushed around just because a couple of research workers had some ends of their own to serve? Would they have to meet the parents *en masse*? Would classrooms be thrown open to them at any time? 'If so, how,' said one teacher, 'can I be expected to carry on teaching with a father in the corner building bookshelves?'

Even more fearfully, others asked whether they would have to commit themselves to several nights' overtime each week. Most of them lived out in the suburbs, and left by car for their homes not long after the children departed. Some were studying in the evenings, or teaching evening classes, and could obviously not contemplate spending a lot of extra time at John Lilburne; these were '9 to 4 teachers' perforce.

Even those without such burdens were still tired at the end of most days. Both teachers and Head had (and have) the sort of days which do not leave them with a lot of energy for extra work.

The Head kept a diary for us of a day at a fairly busy time of the year. It was clear that it would be wrong to expect too much extra work, even from him – though he did in fact somehow manage to do it.

    8.45–8.55 a.m. Preparation of documents required for interviews with parents later in the morning.
    8.55–9.00 Schoolkeeper brought in mail and we discussed his work for the day.

The Changes in the School

*9.00–9.10 Interview with Mr. Solon, a parent whose son has been attending a school for delicate children. Bill is being returned to normal schooling and Mr. Solon was making sure that we could have him back at John Lilburne and that we would make some concessions about P.E. lessons in order to avoid undue strain on the boy.

*9.05–9.20 District Inspector arrived in the middle of the previous interview – an unexpected visit. He was on his way to the office and had dropped in to discuss the ability of a member of staff seeking promotion. We also discussed the arrangements to be made with regard to the replacement of my Deputy Head, who had recently been appointed to a headship.

9.20–9.40 Taking school Assembly.

9.40–10.20 Completion, after consultation with the class teacher, of a confidential report on Betty Arbour required by the Problem Cases Conference at the end of the week.

*10.20–10.30 Telephone call from Mr. Salmon. He had been unable to attend for an interview, but was seeking information about schools with vacancies which were suitable for his son, Timmy. He wanted the boy to attend a school offering only academic courses, and was very upset that the boy had been turned down by the school of first choice.

10.30–10.45 Coffee break in staffroom.

*Called to telephone to speak to tutor from College of Education. A student, Miss Bulgin, had been having a poor practice and the tutor intended to call that afternoon to discuss the question of a possible failure grading. I said I would spend the next period in the classroom with the student to see if there was any advice I could give.

*10.45–11.15 Observation of lesson as promised and discussion with the student.

11.15–11.30 Interview with Mr. Salate about second choice school for his son, Tomas. The boy was suitable for an academic course. Mr. Salate preferred a grammar school, which meant that the boy would have to make a fairly long journey.

*11.30–11.40 Department of Children's Care telephoned to ask what use we made of Voluntary Service Workers in this school, and how did I think they could best be used in

The Changes in the School

primary schools in this area. The person calling was preparing a lecture and required information for that purpose.

11.40–12.00 Talk to children who had not been accepted at school of first choice. The ostensible reason for the talk was to make arrangements for interviews with their parents, but its real value was for me to assure them that their rejection had not been on personal grounds (although in fact in two or three cases it had been so!).

*12.00–12.05 Telephone call from Accounts Section at Divisional Office to check on hours of work of women helpers.

*12.05–12.10 Telephone call from headmaster of local secondary school, who wanted to arrange a convenient morning to come over to see the school and meet some of the boys who would be joining him in September. This call was in answer to a letter I had sent him the previous day, suggesting that he came across during the next week.

12.10–12.15 Interview with Mrs. Harlow for a second-choice school for her son, Michael. Quick and easy, as she accepted the local comprehensive school, where I knew he would be accepted.

12.15–1.25 Lunch-hour
During lunch there was a general staff discussion about secondary school transfers and the reasons why some children had not been accepted at schools of first choice – a general feeling of annoyance at the way in which one or two boys had been treated. This discussion went on after lunch in the staff-room. I had to leave for about ten minutes when the school-keeper brought up the piano repair man, who was searching for a piano which had been reported out of order. After an abortive search he decided he must have been sent to the wrong school.

1.30–1.45 Interview with a prospective part-time teacher, who had been recommended by the head of the Infant Department.

1.45–2.45 Final rehearsal of school play. During this time I told the secretary I was not available for phone calls or interviews except in an emergency, so I was left alone to work with two other teachers on the play.

2.45–3.00 Afternoon break.

The Changes in the School

3.00–3.30 Answering correspondence from morning mail.
3.30–4.00 Discussion with Deputy Head about costumes for school play.
School finished then, but the Head was involved in conversation with members of staff until about 4.30.
* Items in the day which are marked in this way were not planned activities at the beginning of the day.

The daily itinerary of teachers was hardly less trying than that of Mr. Pym. So we were probably not too optimistic in guessing that only four of the teachers were going to be at all enthusiastic, with four the opposite and the other nine somewhere in the middle, waiting to see what happened, more than causing it to happen. Amongst the waverers younger teachers predominated. They lacked confidence in their ability to deal with parents. Parents had not figured in their courses at training college. Several of the older teachers, while very far from lacking confidence, could not see what was wrong with the way they had treated parents (with such evidently good results) in the past. But despite the objections there was eventually a measure of agreement about the four steps we have already listed.

We were also encouraged by the backing of Mr. Phelps, the schoolkeeper, a married man with children in the school. He told us that without him little could be done. 'Outside school hours, the school is my responsibility.' If he'd been awkward there could hardly have been many gatherings in the evenings, and certainly not on Saturdays, though that last is a goal we kept for the most part to ourselves. Luckily for us, he was as enthusiastic as the most enthusiastic teacher. He said he had 'talked to a lot of the parents and they're interested. They'd install floodlights in the playground or build a swimming pool if they were allowed'. He was a valuable ally partly because he lived on the spot, unlike the teachers, and had influence with the parents, people of his own background who went to the same pubs and shops as he did.

The Changes in the School

Two preliminary steps

Before the fourfold programme was put into effect two other preliminary steps were taken. Firstly, the old notice outside the school, which may have been there since Charles Booth for all we knew, was taken down. TRESPASSERS WILL BE PROSECUTED went, and in its place appeared a new notice:

NO ADMITTANCE TO UNAUTHORIZED PERSONS.
PARENTS ARE WELCOME TO SEE THE HEAD TEACHER
AT ANY TIME.
APPOINTMENTS MAY BE MADE IF NECESSARY.

Parents may not have seen the new board. We forgot to ask them. But we certainly saw it, as we climbed the gangplank with our sheaves of paper; we were pleased that the Institute of Community Studies had paid for it. Something had actually happened.

In the second place a letter was sent out from Mr. Pym to all the parents. It was translated into Greek, Spanish, French, Turkish and Italian for the benefit of the main groups of immigrants. It set the tone for what was to follow, and went as follows:

Dear Parents,

From the comments I have received from parents it is very clear that many of you are anxious to know how best you may assist your child with school-work. I thought you might welcome something in writing from me on this point, so that you can study it at leisure and see if it will be of benefit to you.

I must make it clear that I agree with the opinion of the Education Authority that regular homework for young children is neither necessary nor desirable. There are many ways, however, in which school work can be continued in leisure time and developed by parents who are anxious to see their children get the utmost benefit from their education. I have outlined some of these ways below. I know that some of you are already doing many of the things set out in detail.

First, encourage your children to read as much as possible. Let them join the local library and try to assist them to make a

The Changes in the School

suitable choice of books. Friends and relations will probably offer to buy books as presents for the children. Make sure that they get well-produced, attractive editions of the sort you will see in the book exhibition and at the local library. Get the children to read to you – tell them what a word says if they cannot read it and encourage them as much as possible all the time. Help them to look after the books that they borrow or own by putting them in a safe place out of the reach of younger children and pets. Read to the children at times yourself. On these occasions they will enjoy stories that are too difficult to read for themselves.

In the same way, give plenty of opportunities for writing. Encourage them to write to friends and relatives, or to make their own books of stories and accounts of what they have done or seen around them. Avoid formal exercises from textbooks, which do little to encourage lively written work. Take every chance you get to explain new words and the meaning of words that they use. It is surprising how many children are not sure of the meaning of many words that adults take for granted. In the same vein, remember that the spelling may not be as good as you would expect and do not worry about mistakes in spelling in any written work they may show you.

Number work can be improved in children by helping them to think about numbers and quantities in real life. Many games (cards, dominoes, darts, Monopoly, dice games) require accurate counting and calculation. Shopping, weighing and measuring, working out 'rule of thumb' methods used by many craftsmen are all ways in which work with numbers can be made interesting and useful. Very few of us use complicated calculations in real life and it is much better for children to have a sound grasp of small numbers which are within their grasp. Table facts can be learnt by heart and tested as a game. Remember that addition facts: 6 plus 7 equals 13, are as important as multiplication facts: 6 times 7 equals 42.

If you want to encourage your child's work generally allow them to ask questions and show them where they can find the answers for themselves in books, newspapers, etc. Take them on visits to places of interest and discuss with them what they have seen. Encourage them to talk about their work at school and if possible, follow up some of this work themselves. Teachers

The Changes in the School

often throw out suggestions and ask children to see what they can find out for themselves. Help them with this work in every possible way. Give them plenty of chances to draw, paint and make models if their interests lie that way. Avoid 'ready made' models and 'painting by number' kits in favour of things that make the children think for themselves more. Even if they make a hash of doing something it is of value to them. Give them the benefit of your own experience in practical fields – craft work for boys and needlework for girls – but do not expect the standard of work to be high at first.

Television programmes take up much of young people's time today, but these can be very helpful if you choose the programmes wisely and discuss them with the children afterwards. Every child in the school watches a schools' television programme. Some of these are repeated at night or in the holidays. Discuss them with your children. Late-night viewing, even at week-ends, and lack of sleep can hold children back in their school-work. Young children, as you know, need plenty of sleep and you should insist on regular bedtimes, even if this causes arguments at first.

To summarize what I have said so far, the most important thing is your attitude to your children's work. If you show that you are willing to take a regular interest in what they are doing and praise what they can do rather than point out their shortcomings, this will build up their self-confidence, and lead to a marked increase in ability, even in a short time.

If there is any special problem that you have, or any point about your child's work which is bothering you, then come to see me at school. If you let me know in advance, so that I can arrange an appointment, this will save your time and mine. I am willing to see parents at any time in cases of urgency, although I do like to be free from visits between 9.15 and 9.45 in the morning, when I take school assembly.

Yours sincerely,
J. PYM

Open meetings

Now for the main programme. First came the open meetings, on two successive evenings, one for the lower and the other

The Changes in the School

for the upper half of the school. The hall would not hold all the parents at once. A hundred and thirty-two mothers and 72 fathers came to one or the other. Allowing for the fact that some were couples and several had more than one child at school, they represented about 44 per cent of the children in the school. The attendance would no doubt have been higher, as we have already suggested, if the parents could have had a choice of dates, and also if something could have been done about their babies. The Infant School Head was not prepared to organize a crèche for the evening; she was uncertain about her legal responsibility for accidents.

On arriving at the school the parents found their way up one of the turret-like staircases to the second floor, where their names were taken by teachers, who otherwise rather hid themselves away during the meeting proper. One who was unusual, not at all hesitant, began talking right away to one of the fathers she had never seen but whose name she recognized. 'Oh, that's one of my little darlings. He's got the idea he's stupid, you know. It must be you whose given him that idea. He tells me, "My Mum calls me bird-brained." He's not, you know, not at all.' She was not embarrassed; the father was, and shuffled off to pick up a book. For outside the 'hall' were two exhibitions of children's books, one a travelling exhibition prepared for schools by the National Book League and the other of books from a local bookshop. The meetings themselves started with an introduction by Mr. Pym, followed by a talk by a local children's librarian. 'I know that you are all very busy. Many of the mothers as well as having to run a home also have full or part-time employment. But if you can find time to encourage your children to read and join a library you are doing a good job. They need encouragement. There are nowadays so many distractions from reading – TV above all. Children, if they are fond of their parents, like to copy them. The best example comes from the parents. If you read, they will want to. You should at least read *to* them. In this way you can show you enjoy books. As they get older, they will naturally read to

The Changes in the School

themselves. But try to find the time to discuss with them what they are reading.' It was rather too earnest, and many of the parents looked sleepy. When questions began, they perked up.

A first batch, on both occasions, were still about books, and in particular about the school library. Most parents were unsure whether their children could borrow books from it to take home. Although Mr. Pym said they could, this wasn't what had happened. Nor did it seem to for the rest of the year. Parents remained in a muddle about whether books could be brought home, and if so, what was the procedure. For the most part, though, the questions were not about the librarian's talk at all but about the sort of things that, as the last chapter showed, the parents felt most confident about articulating: school meals, the condition of the toilets, the need for a crossing-warden, the parking of cars outside the school and the supervision of children on the staircases when they came in from the playground. A request for a P.T.A. was politely dismissed by the Head. One Cypriot parent on the first evening held the floor for too long with questions which, though cast in a general form, were really about his own son whom he felt had been unfairly criticized by a teacher. There was relatively little about teaching, except for one about the way the timetable was made up and about reading. An Irish father with a thick brogue wanted to know 'Is it still the practice to provide Catholic provision? I ask because our daughter says the "Our Father" different, and gets it mixed up. Then one of the nuns comes along and says, "What's happening here"?' The meeting ended when another father got up to say, 'I would like to thank you for all you have done, and your co-operation with parents.' Despite the thanks, Mr. Pym had a nightmare that night, dreaming of parents pursuing him.

Immediately it was over the parents dispersed individually to their child's classroom, if they could find it, to see the teacher and to make an appointment for a private talk in the following week, either in the afternoon or the evening. Those who did not attend either of the open evenings were sent a letter asking them to say when they could come for a talk.

The private talks

The meeting was only intended to be a curtain-raiser for the private interviews. Some of the teachers were very anxious about them beforehand. The staffroom buzzed. What were they supposed to do? How would they pass a whole quarter or worse half an hour alone with a father or a mother? The advice that could be given to the teachers was only in the most general terms, and we have no direct evidence about its effect. We know that at these private talks about 70 per cent of the families were represented. By the end of the term the figure had risen to 75 per cent. We do not know what actually went on, since we were present at only one of the interviews. This particular one was not too reassuring. Mrs. Chance, the mother, began by commenting: 'One thing that does concern Mary is that she would like to be on top of the class. She has that at the back of her mind often.' Mr. Godden, the teacher, immediately said, 'Well, I don't think she ever will be.' Mrs. Chance flushed hotly at this. 'Oh dear, that's not very encouraging, is it?' Mr. Godden made no attempt to allay her fears, so she went on to ask, 'Would you say she is very fair at English?' 'Yes, but not very marvellous.' We winced almost as sharply as Mrs. Chance.

This may not be typical. We had to rely on what teachers and parents told us afterwards. On the timing, there was general agreement that November was the best time for the talks, long enough after the beginning of the term for the teachers to have got to know their children a little, long enough before the end of the year to enable both teachers and parents to act, if they were going to at all, on the information they had gained from each other while the relation-

The Changes in the School

ship between them had a decent span left to it. There was equally general agreement amongst the teachers that it was a mistake to compress all the interviews into one week, so that teachers had to spend up to four nights in close succession in seeing parents, sometimes as many as ten in an evening.

> 'My head was like a sponge. I hardly knew what I was saying to the last two or three parents I saw.'

The majority of the parents who had attended told us later that it had been worthwhile.

> 'Well, it was nice to see how Billy was getting on without me having to bring the matter up myself. I felt as I was being met half-way.'
>
> 'She really concentrates on Ivor's reading and contacts me if there is trouble. She even came to the house one evening to see me, so that shows she's really interested, doesn't it?'

For their part, the teachers need not have feared there would be any difficulty in passing the time. The parents 'just opened the floodgates'. 'I couldn't stop her.' Most of them thought at the time that they had got something useful out of it – mainly knowledge of the home conditions of particular children – like the child who lived in one room with two grandparents, or the child who lived in another single room with two other children and his parents who watched television after he'd gone to bed. 'When I look at them now I think of all the things I know about them and realize just what some of them have to put up with.' The fullest report was given to us in writing a week or two later by one of the teachers who had been an enthusiast from the beginning.

> 'There were times when, faced with two delightful parents with a thoroughly normal, sociable child I felt like saying, "Well, you are obviously doing your job – I will continue to do mine – I congratulate you on your child. Good evening." These apart, I feel a mixture of satisfaction and irritation, the former far outweighing the slightly jaded effect that the occasional parent

The Changes in the School

leaves with me. On the whole the parents were very happy to come, and grateful too, which is a help. Why is it, I wonder, that fathers seem more aware of the fact that the teacher is doing overtime without the time and a half? Sometimes mothers had to be reminded of the reason for the visit. In one conversation we got as far as "and then I found her naked in bed – the tramp", and Johnny and his reading had hardly figured. With Mr. and Mrs. K., though, I had a most fruitful discussion on the pros and cons of the phonetic and Look-and-Say methods of instruction. Parents were often surprised at the writing ability of their child, saying "Did he copy this? He couldn't have had those ideas himself."

'My blood pressure shot up at one point when a hard-faced woman, holding her daughter's books, said, "I think it's time you learned Maisie to spell properly." Ever since that encounter Maisie has had my deepest compassion. The mother's only complaint was that the child works in school but refuses to dry up after washing the dishes every night. This Mum does not go out to work. Quite a number of things seem to have come out of these meetings. One's sympathy and interest in each child is greatly enhanced – it cannot help but be so. I have one boy who last week was dry at night for the first time in seven years. Dare I possibly hope that my meeting with his mother, and our subsequent action, has something to do with it? In many cases I can see already that more reading is being done at home. Parents of an intelligent but lethargic boy are working hard with me to kindle and sustain his interest. But I feel that parents should be asked to show discretion in their comments at home. I was able to reassure one mother about the progress and behaviour of her son, only to find next morning a little boy puffed up with self-importance. This is the only adverse effect of the interviews I have found.'

Mr. Pym also had few doubts about the value of the interviews. He mentioned particularly the way in which teachers had had to think about the rationale of their classroom methods in order to be ready to explain them to the parents. As for himself, he felt he had formed a relationship with parents that would have taken two or three years to develop if he'd gone on as he had before.

The Changes in the School

Discussions on teaching methods

So much for the autumn term. The third activity for the spring term was to be the smaller discussion meetings on teaching methods. The teachers were more unsure about these than they had been about the individual talks. Most did not at all fancy getting up to expound their methods in front of a bunch of possibly hostile parents, and, still worse, in front of some of their colleagues. The teachers were divided between adherents of the old and new methods of teaching, especially of mathematics, and did not seem anxious to bring their differences out into the open in a way that was likely to cause dissension amongst themselves and disquiet to the parents. A very proper worry also emerged even more clearly at this stage – just what did they want parents to do at home? Not to be an extension of the classroom – the parents were not to be 'teachers' – but if not that, what were they supposed to do?

The meetings had to be restricted to certain years and subjects. The determinant was whether the teachers were willing to take part. The decision was to have four, as follows:

Arithmetic	1st year
Reading	2nd year
Art and Craft	3rd year
Integrated Studies	4th year

Beforehand, 'pamphlets' (or for reading, a 'quiz') were duplicated on each subject and circulated to the parents with children in the appropriate year so that they could read them and get some knowlege of the approach of the teacher concerned before they came. It turned out, though, that these pamphlets[1] were for the most part above the heads of

---

[1] An unexpected outcome was that the reading pamphlet was passed on by one of the parents to a friend who was a teacher in Dublin. She was, according to the report, so impressed that she had decided to introduce 'English methods' into her Dublin school.

the parents, except for the reading quiz. This asked the parents to rate themselves according to the number of 'yes' answers they gave to such questions as 'Do your children have a shelf for their books?' 'When you are out with your children, do you ever ask about words on signs, posters, buses, shops, etc.?', or 'Do you think that, to a young child, the shape of a word is more important than what the letters say?' More appreciated than the pamphlets or the quiz were the easy-to-read newsletters about the school sent out by Mr. Pym.

The first meeting was on arithmetic. Only 15 mothers and 9 fathers came, representing 17 children, or 15 per cent of those on roll for the first year. A display had been mounted, of diagrams and graphs and apparatus in use in the school, such as weighing machines, balances, colour factor sets and counters. None of the parents gave more than a fearful sideways glance at the display during the quarter of an hour given over to a cup of tea before the meeting. They sat stiffly in their chairs, and the teachers likewise. To begin with, Mr. Pym asked the parents what they felt about the pamphlet. They were non-committal and much more polite than they were, later on, when we asked them the same question in their own homes. The atmosphere only warmed up when some of the divisions amongst the teachers became apparent. One of the teachers could at one point be heard at the back, not quite *sotto voce* enough, whispering to near-by parents that 'The good old-fashioned methods were best when you had to learn your tables, and you had to do your sums, and they were either right or wrong'. Another teacher, more outspoken, stood up to declare that children liked nothing more than mental arithmetic, and that it was good for them. This insistence on the need to know tables, immediately taken up by the parents, dominated the discussion. Their demands to know how tables fitted in were never properly satisfied by the adherents of New Mathematics on the staff. Phrases like a 'child's concept of number' were left hovering in the air. Unfortunately, the apparatus

The Changes in the School

was not demonstrated to the parents. Its only value was to the teachers. Some of them had come to look at it in the afternoon, asked questions about it and seemed as though they might be prepared to use it in their own classrooms if they could have it demonstrated. This did not apply to one of the older teachers though. He said after it was all over –

> 'I went to school before anyone in this room, before the First World War, in fact, and we were taught our tables every day – at the end of a stick. We were lined up in front of the teacher and we got them right because we knew if we didn't we would get the stick. And it hasn't done me any harm, has it?'

We did not know. Chekhov also was beaten. It is clearly not only the parents who, as far as teaching methods are concerned, are caught between two worlds.

The following meeting was on Arts and Crafts. The attendance, at 23 mothers and 14 fathers, was higher – a surprise to teachers convinced that parents were primarily interested in the 3Rs. It went more smoothly, partly because the effectiveness of the teaching was demonstrated by the splendid display of children's work on the walls, partly because Mr. Jackson, the teacher in charge on this occasion, was less inclined to press his views and more to let the parents answer their own questions. It was more of a discussion. But once again it was about the virtues of old and new. One father said he thought there was nowadays too much Art and Craft and not enough of the 3Rs. Mr. Jackson not answering, another father came in to disagree:

> 'I don't agree. My son doesn't talk much as a rule about things. But he will talk about Vikings and Danes that he's drawn. He learns more about history than we did with textbooks and lots of dates on the blackboard.'

After a long set-to, Mr. Jackson did finally speak:

> 'It has taken me five years to be convinced that the old methods I used were not the most effective. I was convinced through practice. I'm still changing my ideas as I've changed my ideas about giving talks to parents at meetings like this. A few months

The Changes in the School

ago I resisted the idea strongly and now here I am talking to you about how I teach.'

Many of the parents seemed impressed by the earnestness of his statement. The next meeting was for Integrated Studies, that is for project work involving several subjects. It was less successful, though much more effective use was made of teaching equipment. Attendance was sparse, and the teachers did not encourage the parents to give views as well as ask questions.

The last meeting, though the most poorly attended, was the most lively, this partly because Mr. Pym and Miss Larkin had understood they should not rush in or be so defensive; and partly because the reading quiz supplied a framework for discussion. Some ways in which parents might help – telling stories, encouraging their children to join the library, taking them to the library, listening to them when they want to tell stories, buying them books, letting them have bookshelves, talking to them about items in the paper or on the TV, sometimes reading their comics, asking about signs in the street – were again suggested, as they had been in Mr. Pym's original letter.

Home visits

These were the first three activities. The fourth proposal was that home visits should be made. The intention was that most of the parents who did not respond to the invitations to come to the school should, if willing, be seen at home instead, partly to try and find out why they had abstained. As it turned out, only three of the teachers were ready to do this, and so only 10 homes were visited. A researcher went along on most occasions. Even these few were, however, of some interest. They showed that some of the parents, though they had received bits of paper from the school, had not read them. They were not used to acquiring information from paper. It was only if a representative of the school

The Changes in the School

turned up in person that communication could be established. Misunderstandings could also be removed, as the following account illustrates.

Next to a boarded-up shop the house opened straight on to the pavement. When Miss Marsh (the teacher who came this time) knocked, one of the daughters came to the door and asked us to wait. While we did so, we could catch a sight of the same daughter moving around briskly with a broom. When the sweeping was over we were invited into the living-room. *Coronation Street*, heard only dimly from outside, became almost deafening when we got inside. Even the interior on the telly looked palatial compared to this: a single naked light-bulb hanging on a long cord to shoulder level, a collection of ramshackle furniture including a bed in the corner, and ragged carpet strips over torn lino. Yet it somehow looked comfortable and was now, of course, tidy.

Mrs. Palgrave talked with a throaty cigarette voice. Without any introduction she launched into her marital history up to the point when she couldn't put up with her husband any longer. She didn't work.

'What's the point of working. Anything over 30s. they deduct from the National Assistance, and you've got your fares on top.'

She soon gave at any rate the ostensible reason for keeping her distance from the school. She went to John Lilburne two years before, for an Open Day.

'It was a coloured chap. When I asked to see John's books he said, "How do I know where they are? Look for them." I lost my temper and walked out, and I said I'd never go near the place again if that's the way they treat you.'

After listening to Miss Marsh she changed her mind.

John was throughout not seen but very much heard, making his presence felt by tapping on the window behind us, and later making loud noises from the foot of the stairs. His mother said he was often deaf. There was much speculation, the same as with many much older people than John,

The Changes in the School

about whether he was deaf or just pretended to be, so as not to have to listen to what he didn't want to hear. His noisy behaviour suggested he was speculating likewise about us and perhaps there was some satisfaction in finding out that we apparently were deaf too. Out of politeness we were at any rate pretending to be. Mrs. Palgrave said that the school doctor had examined him a year or two ago and pronounced him not deaf. Mrs. Palgrave did not believe it. Miss Marsh revealed that John had been tested again a few months ago. This was the first Mrs. Palgrave knew of it. The note sent home with John, recording the same negative result, had never arrived, or if it had, it had not been read. His mother had been left in doubt until Miss Marsh arrived.

The immediate outcome of another visit was similar. We did not need to ask why Mrs. Marling had not been to the school. She had four children, all under 10, and no husband. Although harassed by the four of them, she still managed to retain some control. They were not allowed out to play in the street except at week-ends, and were encouraged to draw a lot. A mention of arithmetic produced a collective demand to have some sums set then and there, and for the next half-hour, with the children calculating and scribbling desperately, the teacher put on what we thought was as lively a demonstration of tuition in the home as any parent could hope to witness. Mrs. Marling wondered aloud at the ability of teachers to control children so effectively. Miss Germaine, the teacher, asked the mother to come up to the school and said she would gladly put up with having the younger children along so that Mrs. M. could see Kim's work. An appointment was fixed right away for her to do so.

From another interview a rather different conclusion was drawn. When we arrived at the flat Mrs. Jones was washing Bill's hair in the kitchen sink, his four-year-old sister mooching around below the two of them. The homely scene somehow looked a little bit contrived. Bill smiled very pleasantly at both of us, but especially at his teacher, Mr. Barnes, whom he seemed very glad to see. Mr. Barnes helped

The Changes in the School

in drying Bill's hair, rubbing it very vigorously. Mrs. Jones stood back while he was doing this and said afterwards, a little bit resentfully, 'He would never have let me do that for him.' Then, when he was in his pyjamas, Mrs. J. wondered whether we wanted to see her alone in the kitchen or with Bill. We said that we would rather see her alone, and so Bill went off into the front room, nominally to look at TV.

Mrs. Jones sailed straight in on the topic that we thought she might want to steer clear of.

> Mrs. J.: 'You know what he goes to the clinic for?'
> Mr. B.: 'Yes.'
> Mrs. J.: 'Yes, that's why he isn't going on the school journey this year. It's because of the bed-wetting. He's afraid that the other boys will laugh at him.'
> Mr. B.: 'You don't need to worry about that at all. We're used to it.'

He then explained how they dealt with this problem when they went away on a school journey. She told us about the machine she now had for dealing with Bill.

> 'It lets out a hoot. As soon as a drip of wet is on the sheet it sets the hooter off. It's a cat and mouse game now. Some nights it goes off every half-hour, so I turn it off completely. Last night I didn't hear it and I thought that maybe Bill hadn't done it. But this morning he said to me "Didn't you hear the thing go off?" I hadn't heard it.'

Mrs. J. didn't sound as though she was going to give this new device much of a trial, perhaps rightly.

At various points Mr. Barnes said what a very good reader Bill was. This pleased Mrs. J.: 'He's ever so pleased Mr. Pym gave him a Star. He takes after me. He reads upside-down as well.'

Mr. J. came in and was very keen to know about Bill's prowess at football and very disappointed to hear from Mr. B. that he hadn't got much confidence in spite of his delight in it. Mr. J. was very much more concerned about sports than he was with reading and arithmetic. He said with some

The Changes in the School

pride, almost puffing out his chest, that he had played in some football games in his time.

A small interlude for tea. Questioned whether we liked evaporated milk or cow's milk.

> Mrs. J.: 'Mum and I are always on evaporated milk.'
> Mr. J.: 'I've always been a cow's milk man, and my Mum, too.'

The last subject that came up was money.

> Mrs. J. to Mr. B.: 'Has he been paying the School Fund? I wondered whether he had. We've had a laugh about it. Did he pay this morning?'
> Mr. B.: 'Yes, threepence I think.'

At this point we came to a conclusion, about Bill in the next room and, for that matter, about John, the would-be deaf boy mentioned a moment ago. There is clearly a danger that home interviews of this sort could be used as a way of checking up on a child, who may want for the best of reasons to keep the two halves of his life apart. Does this mean that those who stay away from the school should not be visited? The two previous accounts showed it can sometimes be useful to do so. This is a dilemma to which we will return in the final chapter.

These were the four main features of the trial – there were other lesser ones that we have not reported like the making of a small garden out of rubble. All was compressed into a period of six months in order to be in time for Plowden. Pressure of time gave a sense of urgency. Failing that, years could have passed without very much happening of any kind. On the other hand, the hurry meant that the programme did not grow as it should out of a longer period of discussion with staff and parents.

It is not easy to assess what was done. We could for the most part do no more than gather impressions from parents and teachers, and on some of the activities we have in passing already reported what was said. There was little doubt that the parents were very appreciative indeed of Mr.

The Changes in the School

Pym's efforts, and hardly less so of the teachers'. The highlight of the six months was for most of them the opportunity they had been given of a private talk with their child's teacher. 'The special appointment we had was the first time in four years we had a chance to ask questions', and many of them took advantage to ask them, nearly always about their own particular child. They quite often remembered, too, the advice they had been given, about repeating words rather than pronouncing single letters when helping their children with reading at home, about not getting worried that a child could not yet do £ s. d. sums, or about books to get hold of.

The teachers did not react quite as we expected. As it turned out 3 out of the 15 teachers were sufficiently stirred to throw themselves into it, and one of these was a surprise. He had been categorical at the start that whatever happened he would not want to discuss teaching methods with parents, but after the trial he said:

> 'I suppose when it started I thought of parents coming in and taking over. That's disappeared. Now I feel it is advantageous to know the parents and have them participate in the life of the school.'

One of the others wanted to go even further.

> 'I would like to see more involvement of the parents in school activities, with more opportunity to meet. There should be possibly two or more occasions per month when you tell them you will be there from 4 p.m. to 6 p.m. I have also wondered whether I ought to ask one or two parents about helping with the children's reading – taking two or three children at a time out of the classroom to the library, not only to help them read but to look up works of reference. Parents might also help with organized games.'

All these five considered they had, quite apart from contacts with parents, learnt something of value from the closer communication between themselves and with other teachers that the trial had brought about, and especially from the dis-

The Changes in the School

cussion about methods and from watching the demonstrations given by their fellows.

> 'The main benefit is that one has had to think more deeply about subjects and what others are doing. Mr. Jackson, for instance – I learned a lot from that display of his and the talk he gave.'

For them teaching had become a little less lonely than it ordinarily is. These five were amongst those who were most advanced in their methods of teaching – that is, whose approach was furthest removed from that which the parents experienced when they were children. They therefore had in a sense most need to explain to parents what they were doing. Of the other ten less enthusiastic teachers only one was completely hostile, and only one almost too shy to face parents at all. The others were mostly acquiescent rather than active, some perhaps because the more traditional methods they used were more acceptable to the parents, others perforce because their other engagements outside the school were so demanding.

But at least they were ready, under Mr. Pym's leadership, to continue with the same sort of programme after the trial period was over. Mr. Pym told us that in the following year quite a number of improvements were made. The private interviews in that autumn were spread out over three weeks instead of being concentrated into one. One evening when all teachers were there was set aside for families with several children at the school, and parents were able to move from one teacher to another instead of having to come on different evenings. There was only one meeting on methods of teaching and it was on reading, for the parents of seven-year-olds in the infant school and eight- and nine-year-olds in the junior. It appears to have been much more successful than any of the ones we have reported, perhaps because there were no formal speeches at all. The apparatus and books used in both schools were on display, and the 100 or so parents who came were divided into small groups and taken around by a teacher to show them what everything

The Changes in the School

was used for. Parents were also encouraged to try things out for themselves. Perhaps even more valuable than the evening itself was the meeting that infant and junior teachers held beforehand to discuss how they did teach. Newsletters were continued, and the annual report to parents at the end of the summer term, very much fuller than usual, had a tear-off slip attached for parents to return with their 'report' to the teachers giving another view on how their children had been getting on. At the end of that term Mr. Pym moved on to another job, and since then we have not heard, nor would we expect to hear, from John Lilburne.

5
IMMIGRANTS

To the occasions mentioned in the last chapter all parents were invited. In addition some meetings were organized especially for immigrant parents, who seemed to us in the interviews to be sufficiently different from others to warrant them. We shall try in the first half of this chapter to show why we thought this; in the second half we will describe briefly the action taken.

One of the reasons for choosing John Lilburne was that the numbers of immigrants were not too overwhelming. The need for this was borne in upon us by some of our preliminary visits to the schools in London – Mark Hendon Primary, for instance, a typical nineteenth-century L.C.C. educational block, like John Lilburne, but if anything even less prepossessing. Stacked up in the corner of a high-walled area of grey asphalt, it is in a side street not far from a prison. It is mainly in areas like this, the inner districts along the congested traffic roads into Central London, that the immigrants have settled, packed tightly into rooms above and behind converted shops and into the already overcrowded back streets of decaying Victorian terraces. The very thought of talking to the Headmaster of Mark Hendon about close co-operation with parents seemed an impertinence. To get through another day till 4 o'clock seemed triumph enough.

'Our big problem is just coping with immigrants. We have 42 per cent from overseas, mainly Greek and Turkish Cypriots – there has been some trouble inevitably between them recently – West Indian, Italians (mainly Sicilians), and

Immigrants

so on. I have nothing against them, mark you, but all this talk in Parliament about not segregating them – they don't have to deal with the problem day after day – you have to segregate them. And they resent it. We're teachers and what we want to do is to teach them English first. Many of them don't hear English spoken at all at home. This is the big problem, to get them to hear and speak English continuously. To give you an idea: some of them have run wild in their own country and, you know, urinate in the yard. There was one young girl who, whenever the teacher approached her, would back into a corner, bare her teeth and hiss. She did it to me. That's all we could get from her, just a hiss. So we fetched the medical officer and the girl hissed at him. On investigating, it was found that the girl had been brought up wild in the hills of Cyprus. Just imagine the poor girl's feelings on being suddenly set down here – and the teacher's problem of coping not only with her but with forty-odd other children as well.'

Bank Street Primary is another example. The Head filled in the by now familiar details. 'This was once a lower middle-class area, which has gone downhill. In the last five years there has been a considerable influx of immigrant families. The indigenous families – at least those with initiative – have moved out, leaving us with the poorer, depressed elements. From a roll of 217, 50 per cent are foreigners – not including the Irish.

'Many of the Greek, Turkish and West Indian parents are difficult to get through to. Most of the mothers go out to work. Living in close communities at home and at work, they don't bother to learn English – though some of the fathers do. At the parent interviews for the 11+ choice of school I had to use the children as interpreters. There is one boy of eight who does the official interpreting here and at the clinic.

'The relationship between English and immigrant parents is not too good. The old-established particularly resent the West Indians. The Greeks have some sort of colour bar too.

Immigrants

One Cypriot landlord told a West Indian, "Get back to Jamaica, you're only a foreigner." Inside the school my prime object is to educate them in tolerance, for no academic progress is otherwise possible. I have very little trouble between the children. "Colour" is a word we try to avoid in school, though the West Indians use it. One of the mothers came up to school. An Irish struck a West Indian boy and so the West Indian mother let fly at the Irish boy. All hell broke loose. The woman said, "I don't suppose it will make any difference what I say, because I'm coloured." That's my main problem, to get the children to play and work together.'

At John Lilburne the problem was not as bad as this – or did not seem so to us. When it was possible to communicate – which we did somewhat more successfully later in the longer, more intensive home visits – we found an underlying interest in their children's education. There was little evidence of overt inter-racial tension either. Only a few non-immigrant parents offered unfavourable comments – this although they were in a district in which the notice-boards outside recreation grounds had scrawled over them 'WOGS MUST BE KEPT ON LEAD BY ORDER'.

In the first week of the session at John Lilburne, from a roll of 524 children, there were 152 of immigrant origin – 29 per cent. They were a heterogeneous group: 79 Greek and Turkish Cypriots, 28 West Indians, 20 Italians and 25 from many other countries. Whereas 41 per cent of the immigrant parents had lived in the neighbourhood for less than 2 years, only 9 per cent of the rest of the sample had. Our observations are based on the 34 families (out of 119) in the sample who were all first-generation immigrants, some case studies made by the Institute staff, and a few home visits made by the teachers from John Lilburne. We have in this account somewhat arbitrarily listed four of their 'problems' – housing, language barriers, different educational backgrounds, uprootedness – which in one way or another have a bearing on parent-teacher relations.

Immigrants

(1) *Overcrowding*

Of all the parents, the immigrants were the most difficult to contact, largely because of their long and awkward hours of work and, sometimes, because the family no longer lived at the address known to the school. The majority lived in down-at-heel Victorian terraced houses. Dark, dingy and bare, with no carpets, and mildewed wallpaper, the passageways within seemed to be no one's responsibility. Many of them did not even have light-bulbs. The occupants had neither peace nor privacy in their one- and two-room flats, most of them having to share inadequate toilets and, in some instances, common cookers on staircase landings. Fifty per cent had four or more children compared with 28 per cent among non-immigrants. Frequently we came across large families accommodated in a space of no more than 250 square feet. Many West Indians, as is the custom in their own countries, divided off the room by means of a ceiling-high curtain, one side being for sleeping in. Sometimes without room for two chairs, one of us would have to sit on the bed within touching distance of a television set.

For some of them, whose own education was scanty, the pressures of daily living were such that their own children's progress at school was not exactly at the centre of their concerns. The Langdons, for instance, lived in a dark room which cost them £4 10s. a week. The two-thirds curtained off contained two double beds and one single, the rest cluttered with a few bits and pieces of second-hand furniture. Evon, the boy, had been at John Lilburne for a year; another was still in Jamaica; and Violet arrived from home about two weeks before the interview. The husband answered the questions tolerantly and kindly; Mrs. Langdon could see no point in it, and kept on saying so. Until they were decently housed how could she be expected to worry about what went on in the school? Her plump face, with dark red splotches here and there, was nearly in tears as she waited for the reply. The Benton family lived in two small

Immigrants

back rooms on the ground floor. The rooms were dark, the paint flaking, and the windows cracked. When it rained the lavatory window let in the rain and flooded the interior. There were two beds in one room and a double bed and cot in the other. When we asked Mrs. Benton how they all slept, she said, 'We divide them up between us somehow.' In the evening, all six children sat in one of the rooms from 5-8 p.m. while their mother was out at work, and the father studied in the other room. One son, the subject of the interview, had the job of keeping the others quiet in a room which, when filled by a double bed, was only the size of a passage.

Partly because their housing was so poor many immigrant parents had moved about a good deal since their arrival in London. They had no reason to stay where they were whenever there was a chance of getting something even a little better, and even if the sort of houses just mentioned were an improvement on Cyprus or the West Indies, they were known to be much worse than what many other people in London had. Another reason for movement was that their first jobs were often makeshift, and as soon as they could find one more satisfactory they would seize it, even if as a consequence they had to move to another part of the city. The moving about obviously had an unsettling effect upon the child's schooling, especially if, as sometimes happened, life became so difficult for the family that the child had to be sent back 'home' for a spell. One West Indian girl had, for instance, started at another London Primary School, and then been returned to Jamaica for 18 months before arriving at John Lilburne.

(2) *Language barriers*

Even where the parents had been in the district for long enough to get settled, there was still the language barrier. Why bother to visit the school if you can only nod and smile when you do? Even if their children can translate for them they may not feel they do it too reliably. A Cypriot father at least had enough English to be able to explain that in his view he didn't have enough.

'We don't understand too much English. Next year I may go, as the children can speak more English and I can go to hear them. I am shy to go and ask them (i.e. speak to staff). If I can't understand, all I can say is yes or no. When you go to speak to teachers about your children, it is their whole life; and if you say something wrong it is bad.'

At one door we were confronted with two young Greek Cypriots, strikingly handsome children with jet-black coils of hair and soft brown complexions, who met the opening questions with deferential and smiling incomprehension. 'School – yes – you at John Lilburne?' Louder and more insistent queries eventually brought relations of all ages crowding to the door, including the mother, a heavily-built woman with calloused hands and distracted face. A Cypriot teenager was finally fetched from a house nearby. Whether out of hospitality or a desire to air that essential bit of English he had truly mastered he said, 'Cup of tea, yes?' But, after twenty minutes, no headway was made at all beyond establishing that they had been in England only a few months and that the school was 'good – yes – good'. In their barely-furnished room we smiled, gesticulated and exchanged monosyllabic grunts which were almost drowned by the booming from the corner.

In some households, partly because education was not a woman's business, but also because of her inability to speak English, the mother left the talking to the father (whose own fluency was often almost as limited). They often used the subject of the interview or an older child as interpreter. Half the 34 wives could speak little or no English. Even when the interviewer managed to penetrate the language barrier, he would find himself up against others. Mrs. Kastonis, for instance, who spoke no English, was from a peasant background. Her own schooling had

Immigrants

lasted a mere couple of years. She was unable to comment on teaching methods, because she was unable to grasp what was meant. She could not read Greek, let alone English.

'Oh no, I know nothing about that' was a frequent reply. 'What age did you leave school?' Pause, and a shake of the head as if wondering what could possibly prompt a stranger to put a question like that. One or two questions struck the West Indians as just comical. 'What sort of a job would you like your child to have?' 'Well, of course, I'd like him to have a trade – but . . .' You knew what she meant. Immigrants have few choices. And always the lines of washing everywhere and the children waiting to be fed. Among the West Indians the interview was frequently on the doorstep and sometimes it was impossible to sort out whom the children belonged to, when faced with a bland, defensive wall of incurious courtesy. During one interview the only English a Cypriot husband uttered was, 'Why that fucking Grivas he come?' His son was interpreter, in which role he frequently disagreed with the answers his parents gave.

Allowing for the vagueness in the replies the general impression was that, once having handed over their children at the beginning, relatively few of the immigrant parents had any further contacts with the staff. Of the parents who did, most can hardly have gained much of value from their visits. One father, speaking of an occasion when the mother decided to have a word with the teacher, said:

> 'Yes, she walks straight in and asks for the teacher by name. And the children point the way. She did this a long time ago. You see when you don't speak the language you break the law. But it is not necessary now, as soon as the children can speak the language.'

When asked what happened at Open Day this same parent replied, 'Oh, like a decoration, you know.' It was hardly surprising in these circumstances that, generally speaking, these parents' knowledge of what went on in the school was minimal.

Immigrants

TABLE 3
RESPONDENT KNOWS TEACHER'S NAME

	Immigrant	*Non-immigrant*
Name of teacher known	20%	52%
Name not known	80%	48%
	100%	100%

Similarly nearly twice as many of the non-immigrant parents gave the correct answer when asked whether the children were divided into separate classes according to their ability.

(3) *Different educational background*

Many English parents were confused, as the last chapter showed, by the difference between John Lilburne and the school they had attended when they were children. The immigrant parents were naturally more so. They had to span a gap not just of time but of place. By contrast to their own school back in the villages of Jamaica or Cyprus, the laxness of the discipline was the most mystifying thing.

> 'In my country is very strict. You *got* to learn. When I go to school myself all you can hear is a fly go round. No worse. I don't know how much discipline here. Forty in a class, they talk too much together.'
>
> 'In Cyprus they are forced to do what the teacher tells them.'

There was correspondingly little appreciation of the function of play in learning. As our Greek welfare worker put it to us:

> 'With Greek there is a time for work and a time for play. At home, immediately a child starts school it is expected to be taught to read and write.'

Nor could they understand the refusal to give the children homework, particularly of the formal rote-learning sort which they felt would have enabled them to follow the

Immigrants

progress of the children. Such attitudes were as typical of the West Indians as of the Cypriots. This has also been remarked elsewhere:

> 'The discipline in the (West Indies) schools is strict and the system of teaching is based on book-learning of English books and consists almost entirely of memorizing and rote-learning....'[1]

Nevertheless 31 out of the 32 immigrant parents who gave a definite answer to the question said they thought their children had a better chance than when they were at school.

> 'Sure, yes, they've got more chances because they've got encyclopaedias and what they want; and they've more comics now.'
> 'In my days, my parents never gave me much.'
> 'Yes, in many different ways, the things they learn are far more advanced at school now.'
> 'Oh yes, oh yes. The days of today is more modern than the days of old. In those days the majority of parents had to pay to keep their children at school. You are more or less looked after these days.'
> 'Seem to get more here than we had. They have all these books given them, where we had to find them ourselves.'

Of all the questions asked, those relating to encouragement in the home produced the firmest response from the more settled parents.

> 'Sometimes I give them a certain amount of arithmetic and then check them. And they read to me.'
> 'I always buy her little story books when I go shopping.'
> 'We play games, and if she cannot understand a word she is reading I explain to her.'
> 'They have problems in spelling and reading. They are quite backward. I try to help them, but there doesn't seem to be much improvement.'
> 'I help her mainly in arithmetic, or if she is asking questions

[1] London Council of Social Service. *The Young Immigrant at Home and School*, p.11.

Immigrants

from history or geography, or if she asks something she doesn't know I answer.'

The help they gave was mainly in arithmetic, where the language barrier was less of an obstacle for them. In their ignorance of methods of teaching they were, though, similar to the English parents we've quoted before.

'Yes, the tables. The children will say once two is two, two twos are four, three twos are six. We would say two ones are two, two twos are four, two threes are six. And in arithmetic, when they do the pounds, shillings and pence, when they add it up they put the mark at the bottom when we would put it in the rough column.'

Arithmetic apart, many of the Cypriot parents concentrated on tuition in the Greek language and history. In this they were following the behest not so much of the school as of their Church.

When asked about the kind of thing they did to help their children at home many of the parents were able to give much more confident and detailed answers than they could to questions about what happened inside the school. They knew nothing about parent-teacher co-operation, even of the minimum sort offered in this country through Open Days and other such functions, which might prompt them to take the initiative in seeking advice from the staff. In their own country, even though it was accepted that teaching is the teachers' business and that parents must not interfere, they could nevertheless follow their children's progress through the school and help, if inclined, because nothing very much had changed since their own schooldays. Over here, where education was merely one of a number of strange and bewildering aspects of English life which they found difficulty in adjusting to, they did not visit the school because they were unaccustomed to being given an opportunity to do so. The interest was there, but the means to develop it were not clear to them. More than one interviewer commented on their 'wanting to know how their children

Immigrants

were getting on at school, but not knowing how to go about it'.

(4) *Uprootedness*

Since all of the immigrants we interviewed were first-generation, all the children were growing up within a different cultural environment from their parents. Whereas for the parents the present was filled with memories of the past, for the children it was the moving-off point into the future. It was partly this lack of identification with British customs and traditions which their children were absorbing with less conscious effort that discouraged the parents from seeking to meet the staff of the school, which appeared to some of them to be the instrument for alienating the second generation from the first. This disparity and distance between the two was particularly marked in families where the parents spoke little or no English. The Karatis family, for instance, where the father was voluble, in his own language, only when he talked about the four centuries before Grivas, when Greeks and Turks lived in harmony. His son, Petros, asked as intermediary, did not seem to know much about his parents. He needed to find out their ages and jobs.

All were to some extent uprooted; the Cypriots more so. Their frequent lack of understanding of the school reflected not only the marked difference between the parents' own schooling and their children's but also the sharp contrast in family structure. We would confirm from our own very limited observation that

> 'In Cyprus . . . the father, as head of the family, was usually a strict disciplinarian . . . and he often employed corporal punishment for misbehaviour. . . . Girls were not allowed to mix with boys and it was considered a stigma in the family if a girl was found to have a boy-friend.'[1]

[1] London Council of Social Service. *The Young Immigrant at Home and School*, p.4.

Immigrants

Hence their criticism of John Lilburne for its permissiveness, and their firmly rooted objection to co-education.

It is perhaps even more confusing for the child, eager to be accepted by his own age group and therefore tending to conform in manners, habits, customs and speech while outside the family only to find on returning home that he may incur the displeasure or wrath of his parents through the very fact of his becoming 'anglicized'. As one Greek mother said of her daughter, with a mixture of satisfaction and regret:

'Androulla, she *English* really.'

The insistence on the part of most Cypriot parents that their children learn Greek in the evenings was one way of ensuring that the past was remembered.

At the same time most of the parents wanted them to get everything they could out of the school.

> 'The Headmaster he spoke to us and about Michael – how he is at school, and show us the book, and say he speak very good English – very good writing. I stay in London for my boys they finish their school which is good' (Greek Cypriot).
>
> 'I would like them to stay on at school as long as they can stay' (West Indian).

Despite the ambivalence of parents many of the children were succeeding, in a way not open to the older generation, in adapting themselves to England. The most striking example was a Cypriot girl we met who had gone on through English schools until she was now taking A levels with the intention of becoming a teacher. She explained that in her opinion she had come just in time. 'I had a very good teacher who used to give us special tuition during breaks, at lunchtime, and after school. She told me I could get to the top. At eleven this is more important, when your ideas are just beginning to change. If I had come over at 15 I would have been Greek and it would be too difficult for me to become English.

'My parents have always supported me. We can use the

Immigrants

dining-room to study quietly. And, if I ask, my father is always willing to give me the money for books. In most Greek homes the father is the dominant one. In some, he is a bully. But in my family they are more equal. Though my parents are strict they are tolerant. As I am learning French they let me go to Paris on a school trip. As long as you show good results they will allow you to do things.

'Most Greek parents feel they are not educated enough to understand what goes on in the school. On the last Prize Day I didn't know whether to ask them, particularly as my mother would not understand what was being said. But she came, and my little brother translated bits of it to her. She sat there for three hours. I thought she would be bored, but she said it was marvellous. At Open Days both my parents come. But they do not know much about the school. For the rest, my father trusts me.'

Although rather to our surprise, almost the same proportion of immigrant parents as of the other parents responded to the Head's invitation to visit the school and see their child's teacher, few of them seemed able to talk coherently to the teacher or follow the discussions on teaching methods that took place at later meetings. It was decided to hold special meetings for the two main groups of immigrants, Cypriot Greeks and West Indians. There was some misgiving about separating off this second group from the native-born since they might feel sensitive to any kind of discrimination. The Greeks, on the other hand, seemed to stress their own identity as a separate community and welcome recognition of it. This may partly account for the differing attendance.

Only 4 West Indian mothers and fathers attended the meeting and were reluctant to express any criticism of the school until Mr. Pym, the Head, asked what they thought of the discipline. 'I believe in beating', 'Children should be scolded properly', were the predominant sentiments. After an hour and a half, though the parents were still disinclined to accept the Head's views on discipline, homework and

Immigrants

teaching methods, they were perhaps able to see that the teachers were really trying to do what they thought best for the children.

For the Greek parents' meeting the classroom was packed with 25 mothers and 10 fathers, some of the older women in black peasant shawls. The men were the spokesmen and they needed little prompting to voice their criticisms. There was a noisy and gesticulating exchange of opinion about co-education (against), play (against), homework (for, why didn't the school give it?) discipline (not severe enough). At the end four mothers volunteered to translate letters to and from the school. It had been known all along that the school would get nowhere without arranging for translation – which is why, after the initial letter already quoted, Mr. Pym, the Head, had agreed to arrange for all his letters to parents to be translated into the appropriate languages which meant in practice, French, Spanish, Italian, Greek and Turkish. (The Indian languages proved too difficult for the time being.) This, we found on subsequent visits, was very much appreciated by the parents.

Home visits

Although the Greek parents' meeting could be counted a success, it had still only attracted a minority. We were faced with the same question as we were with the rest of the native-born parents. Was anything to be gained from home visits? Two groups of children were chosen for these visits. The first group of 12 was drawn from 9–11 year olds, the second group of 11 were all in their first year of junior school and were in a special class, smaller than usual, designed to give extra attention to children who were behind in their school-work. Most of the families were visited twice, sometimes three times.

Wherever necessary we took an interpreter in order to avoid the usual situation of a child being used to interpret, often enough the very child whose problems at school we

Immigrants

had come to discuss. These interpreters were drawn for the most part from local people. They had as much to teach us as the people we visited about what to avoid as well as not to. A Cypriot shoemaker who bore a card saying 'Official Interpreter in Legal & Welfare Cases, Greek and Italian spoken', made it plain that to him the mothers in the homes visited should not meddle with high affairs of education. We did not accept his view, though the behaviour of some of the wives – dressed in black, standing respectfully by while their husbands talked of these grave matters – showed that it would be unwise of the school not to take account of this attitude.

For these visits the full questionnaire that had been given to the sample of parents drawn from the whole school was not used. Instead a much shorter questionnaire was prepared, designed to find out how long the children had been in England, what schooling they had had, how many times they had moved house, what their living conditions were like and their parents' jobs and education. We tried to encourage the parents to talk as freely as possible about their views on education and John Lilburne school in particular, and above all to discuss anything that was worrying them about their child's schooling. One of our aims was (with the parents' permission) to report back to the school on particular problems that might be solved and in this way to act as unofficial 'liaison officers' between home and school. We spent some time observing the children in the classroom so that we would know a little about them when we met their parents. Perhaps the best way to illustrate the kind of difficulties parents were faced with is to describe a selection of them in detail.

George. George's father is a Greek Cypriot with his own business, his mother Welsh. They own the house they live in but keep only three back rooms for themselves. The rest is let. They have been backwards and forwards to Cyprus several times. George has had two changes of school in

Immigrants

England and has also had to cope with changing from I.T.A. back to the ordinary alphabet. Mrs. Kasani waded in at once:

> 'Well, you know what I think, what the doctor's told me, it's the school that's caused George's asthma. It's only started since he went up to the Juniors. He's missed ever so much school since then. He doesn't want to go.'

George had in fact missed the greater part of the term. The slightest hint of rain or fog in the air and he was kept at home for fear of an attack of bronchitis or asthma. Mrs. Kasani's real complaint seemed to be that the children were forced to go out into the playground at breaks unless it was actually snowing or raining. She felt sure this aggravated George's bad chest. The family doctor had encouraged her to put the blame for George's asthma on the school – it was a convenient scapegoat. His own and his mother's anxiety had combined to give George a mild case of school phobia. The less he went the more he feared to go.

> 'The children are so rough and he's got no friend to play with. He's got a Greek cousin there with a bunch of friends but they won't have anything to do with George because he's only half Greek.'

George was very behind at school-work, shy and diffident but anxious to please. His father was mainly concerned with his learning Greek. He always spoke Greek to his three children and George and his sister had two hours Greek lessons every week. The interviewer suggested that Mrs. Kasani should get a letter from her family doctor about George's health and go and discuss her worries with Mr. Pym. (She had so far made no attempt to see him.) With George's special problems he would be unlikely to refuse permission for him to stay in the classroom at break. And so it proved. George now sits playing peacefully at break-time and has made a friend. He has even asked if he can go out to play with the other children when it's sunny. He has hardly missed any school since.

Immigrants

Antonis. Antonis, very good looking with a delightful way of wrinkling his nose when he smiles, also has Greek lessons at the church school twice a week. Though they have lived here 20 years Mrs. Valides speaks no English at all. Her husband didn't seem to think this odd:

> 'She would like to learn but she is always too busy with too much to do at home.'

Busy she certainly is, with 10 children, 7 of them still living at home. Antonis is much the youngest. Mr. Valides had to keep referring to his wife for the answers to questions, particularly the ages of his children – he seemed to have lost count:

> 'When you start a family you don't intend to have so many. But then they come and with God's help we manage. Our church teaches that to stop children coming is to live in sin.'

Antonis's schooling is disrupted every summer when they move to join relations. He also attended a different Infant school so he has had six changes since he began. He watches television every night till nine with all the family. Mr. Valides had made a few attempts to help him with reading but in the same room as the television and he complained that Antonis would not concentrate:

> 'I think he's lazy.'

He had thought vaguely of sending him to boarding school.

> 'But will they take boys who wet the bed?'

Mr. Valides has a job that takes him away too much of the time for him to concern himself with his children's needs. He leaves that to his wife and she, of course, cannot visit the school because she speaks no English. An appointment was arranged for him with Mr. Pym who suggested he leave Antonis at John Lilburne for the summer terms instead of removing him to another school. Mr. Pym felt he was too young for boarding school at eight and advised against it. Mr. Valides did as he suggested.

Immigrants

Paul. Paul, from Mauritius, is a fidget at school and Mrs. Touri says he is a terribly nervous child, always rushing from room to room:

'I say him, what matter with you? You got needles you bottom?'

She is struggling with the intractable problem of his bed-wetting. Whatever technique she tries, being cross, being understanding, lifting him at night, giving him special pills from the doctor, nothing has any effect. He is usually put to bed at 8 but is still awake at 11.

'Those tablets make sleep go away. I think no come back no more.'

She says the bed-wetting makes her nervous and upset.

'I fight with my husband about this. I say, "Why not take him one specialist, maybe he do something."'

They have only two rooms to live in, a rather grand front room with family photographs and a map of Mauritius on the wall, and a bedroom where parents and two children sleep and the wife also has to cook. Mr. Touri was very concerned that Paul was behind at school (French is always spoken at home) and was anxious to do all he could to help. If Paul did any reading at home to catch up his father gave him 2s. 6d.! It was suggested that he might like to discuss with the class teacher ways in which he could encourage Paul and that he should see Mr. Pym to ask for the boy to be referred to the enuretic clinic. This he did.

These examples have been chosen because they illustrate the main problems mentioned in Part I – overcrowding, the language barrier, a different educational background and the uprootedness from which so many immigrant children suffer. There were also cases in which the interviewer, acting as 'liaison officer' with the school, was able to suggest some positive action and bring about a closer relationship between home and school. In so many other cases, particularly where overcrowding was the main problem, there was

Immigrants

little to be done to alleviate an intolerable situation. It was admirable that these families kept going as families at all, that the children appeared at school so regularly each morning dressed in clean clothes and full of energy. Particularly interesting, in this context, are Mr. Pym's remarks after one of the home visits he paid:

> 'The main benefit to me from this evening was an appreciation of the living conditions of the child, together with an awareness of the very long working hours of these people as with so many immigrants.'

Conclusions

On the basis of the Head's reactions and those of other teachers it seemed that visits to the parents' homes were worthwhile in creating a much greater understanding of the children's backgrounds and difficulties. Where parents could be persuaded to come to the school and talk, through an interpreter if necessary, long-standing problems could often be cleared up.

One of the greatest handicaps for many of the immigrant children seemed to be that they never heard English spoken at home and their mothers could not help or encourage them with school-work at all. So many of the parents we spoke to said they would like to learn English that an attempt was made to start an English class for them at a local evening institute. In the event only one man turned up and the class was discontinued. It seemed that with young children to look after and fathers who worked long hours, some at two jobs, it was virtually impossible for immigrant parents to come out to regular classes. We felt that had the class been held in the school itself, possibly during school hours, some mothers might then have attended. But even better would be basic English tuition on a one-to-one basis in their own homes. If mothers, in particular, could learn even a little English they might feel less cut off from the new world into which their child was moving and encourage him

Immigrants

to participate in it more fully. English classes for Asian mothers have in fact been run successfully at Spring Grove School, Huddersfield.[1]

Above all, we felt from our evidence that there was a strong case to be made for 'immigrant liaison officers' to be attached either to a single school, if it were large enough to warrant it, or to a group of schools. So many difficulties seem to arise because parents have no previous knowledge of English education and expect the school to use the same methods of teaching and discipline as they themselves experienced in Barbados or Cyprus 20 years ago; or, for that matter, because the teachers never see for themselves the appalling conditions of overcrowding that some of their pupils face when they return home each day.

Immigrant parents are among the more enterprising and talented of the people in their home countries who have uprooted themselves partly for the sake of their children's future. Their children are likely to be above average in intelligence (to judge by studies of other migrant groups). Some of the examples we have just given show how much failure in communication there is between home and school and how worthwhile it would be to try and improve it so that immigrant children could, alongside the native born, make full use of the educational opportunities that could be theirs.

[1] Burgin, T., and Edson, P., *Spring Grove - The Education of Immigrant Children*.

6
TESTS OF EDUCATIONAL PERFORMANCE

THERE are several different ways of assessing the changes made. The opinions of teachers and of parents both count, and we have referred to them in Chapter 4. So even more would the views of the children if only we had managed to devise means of obtaining them. There is another method which is worth trying even though it is a good deal more stringent than what is done with most educational innovations; it is to try and trace out the effect of parental involvement upon the children's educational performance as measured by conventional tests, limited as these are. We knew that even for the tests we used we would not be able to relate cause and effect with any precision, in other words to demonstrate that particular changes in performance were the result of the action taken with parents. An experiment of the kind used in testing the efficacy of the Initial Teaching Alphabet would have been necessary for precision, and that we had to rule out for the reasons given in the opening chapter. We fell back on a case study instead, though we did pick two schools near to John Lilburne as 'controls' of a sort. All the same, it was worth making what measurements we could. Although we would not be able to prove that parental involvement did raise the children's performance we might be able with the aid of measurement to support, or to modify, the impressions we had formed from our talks and observations about the outcome of the changes made.

All the children at John Lilburne were tested in the autumn of 1965, just before the trial period described in

Tests of Educational Performance

Chapter 4, for a second time six months later and for a third time a year later in the autumn of 1966. The tests used were again the ones already mentioned – two of intelligence, of Verbal IQ and Non-Verbal IQ, and two of attainment, in arithmetic and reading.

The changes in scores over the first six months are set out in Table 4. Children in general naturally do better on the tests as they grow older. But the tests used have been tried out by the people who created them (as referred to in Appendix 1) to see how much improvement there is on average with large samples of children as they get older.

The children at John Lilburne may not be the same as the children in these samples. But in so far as they are, the schools where the tests were standardized for age act as controls. We can estimate from them how much improvement there should have been at John Lilburne merely because the children were six months older, and make adjustments accordingly. If the unadjusted scores of the children at John Lilburne had been raised by exactly the same amount as children in general who were six months older the adjusted score in Table 4 would have been zero. As it is, the adjusted scores say for reading had improved by 1·56, which means when translated into months that in 'reading age' the children had gained 3·2 months more than children in general.

TABLE 4
AVERAGE DIFFERENCES IN SCORES
OVER SIX MONTHS' TRIAL PERIOD FOR CHILDREN AT
JOHN LILBURNE

	Verbal	Non-verbal	Reading	Arithmetic
Average differences in children's scores	+0·76	+5·83	+1·56	+3·01
Numbers of children taking tests before and after trial	442	448	438	454
Level of statistical significances	Not	0·1%	0·1%	0·1%

Tests of Educational Performance

Table 4 shows that the changes were all in the right direction, upwards, and those in Non-Verbal, Reading and Arithmetic were all statistically highly significant.

The tests were also repeated at the end of a further six months. If there had been a return to the original levels once the trial period was finished this would have suggested that nothing of more than passing value had been gained. The results in Table 5 show, however, that at the end of a year the improvements of the first six months had on the whole been maintained. The figures for the first six months are different from those in Table 4. This was because before the second six months was up about a quarter of the children had moved on to secondary schools.

TABLE 5

AVERAGE DIFFERENCES IN SCORES DURING FIRST AND SECOND SIX MONTHS FOR CHILDREN AT JOHN LILBURNE

	Verbal	*Non-verbal*	*Reading*	*Arithmetic*
Average differences in children's scores over first six months	1·75	4·16	1.89	3·07
Level of statistical significance	Not	0·1%	5%	1%
Average differences in children's scores between first and second 6 months	2·64	4·33	0·33	—0·99
Level of statistical significance	0·1%	0·1%	Not	Not
Number of children taking tests on all three occasions	283	225	286	293

It does not follow that the improvements over the first six months, generally maintained as they were in the second six months, were necessarily the result of parental involvement, or indeed of anything else that happened in the school except for the testing itself. The improvement might only have been an artefact created by the effect of practice. In our case study we had to use the same, or similar tests for the same children both before and after the trial period. If we had used different tests no meaningful comparisons could have been made. But the children might have done better when they took the tests the second time merely because they had taken them before. An alternative design would have been to start in Year 1 by testing only the fourth-year children before initiating changes in the school, and to test fourth-year children in Year 2 and in later years. No children would then have taken the tests more than once. But this design has serious disadvantages too. It would be no use only continuing for two years in one or a few schools since there might be large differences in the ability or other characteristics of the fourth-year children in successive years and one would not be able to check on the ability of the children before action was taken to involve parents without giving them the same tests twice. It would be necessary to continue for several years in order to even out over time differences between children. But if that were done the school (or schools) would almost certainly change in other vital respects – for instance, in the composition of the staff. Even if we had preferred this alternative design it would have had to be ruled out because we wanted to finish before it was too late for the Plowden Report. We were therefore forced to put up with the disadvantages of repeating the tests.

We did this less reluctantly than we might otherwise have done because the effects of practice had been investigated previously in primary schools by Watts, Pidgeon and Yates. Both coaching and practice raised performance in four tests very similar to those we employed, including a Non-Verbal one; but the effect did not seem to last for long. 'Our evidence supports the view that the effects of coaching and practice cannot be expected to persist beyond a period of a few months'[1] Since at John Lilburne school the

[1] Watts, A. F., Pidgeon, D. A., and Yates, A., *Secondary School Entrance Examinations*, p. 16.

interval was six months, this evidence would suggest that over such a period practice would not have made much difference.

But one clearly cannot exclude it and we thought this the more when the results were produced, as they have now been in Table 4. The most striking increase was in the scores on the Non-Verbal test. It is plausible to believe that if a child had never seen such a thing before the first such paper was put on the table, the benefit of having had one try might be considerable. With Arithmetic or Reading (or even with the Verbal test) where the children were doing exercises anyway in the ordinary course of school-work which were somewhat similar to the tests we used, the value of practice might be less. With Non-Verbal (as well as Reading) we had also to repeat exactly the same test since there was no suitable alternative form, so that for that reason too practice might on these two have mattered a good deal.

Further schools added

The doubt was there anyway, and this led us after the figures for the first six months at John Lilburne had been tabulated to bring in two 'control' schools. These could not whatever we did be satisfactory for the purpose. There can never be a complete matching of any one school with another. Schools are never that alike. Nor can individual children in one school be confidently matched with individual children in another school or schools unless one knows that the differences between the schools are slight. It is only when one begins not with one school but with a random sample of experimental schools (with differences between them randomized) that one can then properly select in an identical manner a random sample of control schools. But still it seemed worthwhile to gather additional information about children in *somewhat* similar schools which might throw light on the extent of the practice effect. If the rise in scores in these other schools was non-existent or much smaller than at

Tests of Educational Performance

John Lilburne that would suggest that the practice effect was not so important after all.

We chose two other junior schools nearby, which we call Thorne and Fenton, with about the same proportions of immigrants and with the same sort of social class composition. We asked the two Heads if they would allow their children to be tested twice at six-monthly intervals. This they agreed to do. We did not think it would be right to conceal in any way from the Heads why we needed their co-operation or ask them not to make any marked changes in their schools during the six months. Since the interests of children must obviously always take precedence over the interests of research, it would have been wrong to dissuade the Heads from making any changes they thought would help the children for whom they were responsible. Hence, but very properly, our undoing. The results of the tests in the two schools are compared with those at John Lilburne in Table 6. The increases at Thorne in the Verbal, Non-Verbal and Reading tests, and the decrease in Arithmetic, were all statistically significant, as were the increases at Fenton on Non-Verbal and Reading. There were no statistically significant differences between Thorne and Fenton when taken together on the one hand and John Lilburne on the other except, markedly, in Arithmetic.

TABLE 6

AVERAGE DIFFERENCES IN SCORES DURING A
SIX-MONTH PERIOD AT JOHN LILBURNE AS
COMPARED WITH FENTON AND THORNE SCHOOLS

	Verbal	Non-verbal	Reading	Arithmetic
Average differences in scores at John Lilburne	+0·76	+5·83	+1·56	+3·01
Numbers of children	442	448	438	454
Level of statistical significance	Not	0·1%	0·1%	0·1%

Tests of Educational Performance

TABLE 6 continued

	Verbal	Non-verbal	Reading	Arithmetic
Average differences in scores at Fenton	+0·07	+7·22	+1·48	−0·24
Numbers of children	201	214	196	213
Level of statistical significance	Not	·1%	5%	Not
Average differences in scores at Thorne.	+1·26	+6·49	+1·64	−1·39
Numbers of children	293	299	280	288
Level of statistical significance	5%	0·1%	1%	0·1% (reduction)

But the similarities between the three schools do not necessarily mean that the rises must be attributed to practice effect alone. We went back to each school to find out if there had been overt changes during the six months. The Head of Fenton said he had no sooner seen and copied the first round of test scores than he had presented them to the Divisional Office of the I.L.E.A. (as it had by then become) in support of a plea he had already made for additional teachers. Whatever doubts we may have had about the tests he did not share them. His case was that his children's performance at reading and arithmetic was clearly below their capacity as revealed by the two 'intelligence tests', and it was accepted. He was immediately given two extra part-time teachers, one a Cypriot to concentrate on small groups of less able immigrant children, the other an English teacher to devote himself to the English children shown up by the tests as the most backward, and especially to those whose 'intelligence' results were relatively good. The two part-time teachers and indeed all the full-time teachers were asked to go all out to improve reading before the six months was up. The Head was very pleased with the response of his teachers. They had realized they had 'promising material to work with'. The reading age of a number of children was pushed up by two or three years. Much the same had happened at Thorne. The

Tests of Educational Performance

Head had not obtained extra teachers but he had drawn up and introduced a new scheme for teaching reading.

'It is a better way of utilizing the existing reading books in the school. I have graded all the books into age ranges of six months and have prepared work cards attached to each book. We have discussed this scheme at great length and of course the teachers knew the children were being tested. I think this might account for the improvement in reading.'

As the second lot of tests results seemed to indicate that his reading scheme had worked, but possibly at the expense of arithmetic, he was now proposing to draw up a similar plan for arithmetic.

Although worth reporting to illustrate the unintended effects of research,[1] the outcome at these two additional schools does not, to say the least, lend itself to an easy interpretation. The most obvious is that the deliberate effort made to improve reading ability by means of ordinary classroom teaching at Fenton and Thorne did work, and did so about as effectively as the attempt to do the same thing by less ordinary means through the involvement of parents at John Lilburne. Neither Fenton nor Thorne did anything special about arithmetic whereas John Lilburne did as part of its programme for working with parents, and at the two former there was a fall or no increase in arithmetic scores while at the latter there was quite an improvement. The results at Thorne and Fenton also suggest, without by any means proving, that practice effect was not the only influence operating. If it had been, arithmetic scores would not have been lower at Thorne. But the upshot at Thorne and Fenton does also further support the supposition we have already made about John Lilburne, that practice played an appreciable part in the rise in the Non-Verbal scores. It can be no

---

[1] The Hawthorne Effect is used as a general term to describe the influence any social science research may have in increasing the enthusiasm and performance of its subjects. (See Mayo, E., *The Human Problems of an Industrial Civilization*.) What we have reported is a particular type of Hawthorne Effect which perhaps deserves a name of its own to denote the stimulating influence of a mere test upon later performance. Perhaps 'Bethnal Green Effect' would be an appropriate term.

Tests of Educational Performance

more than supposition because the two additional schools can as we have seen not be considered as strict controls.

This experience also sharply raises a further uncertainty about the results. The apparent improvements at John Lilburne may have been due, as at the other two schools, not to closer parental involvement but to the enthusiasm aroused amongst the teachers by the research project. They may have consequently become more effective teachers. Some of them certainly said they had learnt from each other as the result of all the discussion of methods in and out of the staffroom. Whether they learnt anything or not, they may also have been stimulated by knowing that the tests were going to be repeated. We could not, however, measure the quality of teaching methods nor the spirit with which they were employed, either before or after the trial, and for that reason we cannot be sure how far the teachers did produce directly, and not indirectly through the parents, any improvement there may have been.

Differences within the school

All that we have been able to show so far in this chapter is that there were improvements in performance at John Lilburne taking the school as a whole but without being sure how far practice and/or better teaching were responsible for them. The other approach open to us is to contrast children with each other *within* the school, and to do so by comparing them according to what their parents did.

Before we get on to family involvement we should, however, say something about other differences between children considered on their own. For the purposes of analysis we naturally compared children in all ways we could think of. The differences between them were not for the most part related to changes in their test scores. Girls improved as much as boys, the older children as much as the younger, children of manual workers as much as the rest. What was perhaps more striking was that there were no appreciable

Tests of Educational Performance

differences between immigrant children and others, as Table 7 shows. Only on the Verbal test was the difference at all statistically significant. One would expect immigrant children to do better on the Arithmetic and Non-Verbal tests where proficiency in the language matters less.

TABLE 7
AVERAGE DIFFERENCES IN SCORES DURING FIRST SIX MONTHS FOR IMMIGRANT COMPARED WITH OTHER CHILDREN

	Verbal	Non-verbal	Reading	Arithmetic
Immigrants	−0·85	6·15	1·27	2·50
Numbers	108	117	106	119
Non-Immigrants	1·29	5·71	1·65	3·19
Numbers	334	331	332	335
Level of statistical significance	5%	Not	Not	Not

We were also interested to know whether the children who had been doing less well before the trial improved more than others. One cannot for this purpose legitimately isolate the children with low scores on individual tests taken one by one since these children would anyway be expected for statistical reasons to rise towards the mean for the school when retested, just as the children with high scores would be expected to fall. Another measure of 'performance' is given by comparing scores on attainment tests with those which to a somewhat larger extent assess potential ability. We did, for instance, label children whose Arithmetic scores were lower than their Non-Verbal scores by six or more points as 'large under-achievers', those where the scores were lower by five points or less as 'small under-achievers', and those whose Arithmetic scores were correspondingly higher than their Non-Verbal as large or small over-achievers. It turned out that the average scores in each of the categories were more or less the same for Arithmetic although not for Non-Verbal. The results are given in Table 8. The downward trend in Arithmetic scores was statistically highly significant. More or less the same result was given by making the same comparison for the Verbal and Reading Tests. The conclusion is that the children who apparently benefited most from the new régime at John Lilburne were those whose achievement had previously fallen below their potential.

TABLE 8

COMPARISON OF THE UNDER-ACHIEVERS AND OVER-ACHIEVERS IN ARITHMETIC

	Large under-achievers	Small under-achievers	Same	Small over-achievers	Large over-achievers
Numbers of children	149	72	11	78	137
Mean improvements in Arithmetic scores over first 6 months	6·38	2·28	5·00	2·12	0·04
Average scores on first Arithmetic test	90·41	90·29	89·82	91·69	95·68
Average scores on first Non-Verbal test	104·15	93·12	89·82	88·55	83·69

Parental participation

So far we have not in this chapter taken account of the crucial question of how parents reacted. We tried to do this in two ways, by finding out from the parents in the sample what changes if any they had made at home during the trial and by recording which parents came to the school in response to the invitations from Mr. Pym. The first was a failure. The numbers in the sample were not in general large enough to produce statistically significant associations with the changes in the children's performance.[1] If we were starting again on another case study in a single school we

[1] The only firm conclusion reached from a further regression analysis was a negative if important one, that the children who improved most were not the ones whose parents had, as judged in various ways before the trial began, taken the most interest in their children's education.

Tests of Educational Performance

would endeavour to interview all the parents both before and after the trial.

We therefore had to rely on such analysis as we could make of all the parents. They were invited, as we have seen, to come to the school for an individual talk with the class teacher. The majority of mothers responded, and a minority of fathers. The relationship between their attendance and changes in their children's performance is set out in Table 9. The only statistically significant differences between children according to whether their mothers attended or not were for Reading. Fathers' attendance did not make any difference. The differences on the Reading test between children who had one or other parent attending, or neither attending, merely reflect what mothers did on their own.

TABLE 9

RELATIONSHIP BETWEEN ATTENDANCE AT PRIVATE INTERVIEWS AND MEAN DIFFERENCES IN SCORES OVER THE TRIAL PERIOD

	Verbal		Non-Verbal		Reading		Arithmetic	
	Nos.	Diffs.	Nos.	Diffs.	Nos.	Diffs.	Nos.	Diffs.
Mothers attending	305	* 1·28	308	** 5·98	300	** 2·36	310	** 3·39
Mothers not attending	137	−0·38	140	** 5·49	138	−0·18	144	** 2·19
Fathers attending	102	* 2·21	103	** 6·95	101	−1·76	106	** 2·40
Fathers not attending	340	−0·33	345	** 5·49	337	** 1·50	348	** 3·20
Either parent attending	343	** 1·29	347	** 5·98	338	** 2·07	351	** 3·20
Neither parent attending	99	−1·07	101	** 5·30	100	−0·17	103	** 2·35

Mean differences between scores on the first and second test which are marked with one asterisk are significant at the 5% level; those with two asterisks at the 1 per cent level or higher. The rest are not significant. The only statistically significant differences between the pairs, e.g. mothers attending or not attending, are noted in the text.

Tests of Educational Performance

The same conclusion stands out about attendance at the meetings for parents of the first-year or second-year children. Table 10 refers to the Reading meeting. The children whose mothers or fathers came all did significantly better than those whose parents did not. One reason for the difference between second-year children and others may be that all parents of that year, whether or not they attended the meeting, received written advice from the Head about ways of helping their children at home. Attendance at the Arithmetic meeting did not seem to matter to the same extent. This rather confirms our impression that the reading meeting had been on the whole better run by the staff than the arithmetic meeting.

TABLE 10

RELATIONSHIP BETWEEN ATTENDANCE OF PARENTS AT READING MEETING AND CHANGES OF SCORES OF THEIR CHILDREN ON READING TESTS, COMPARED WITH NON-ATTENDING PARENTS

	Numbers	Mean Differences in scores
Second-year Mothers attending	11	+11·54**
Second-year Mothers not attending	84	+2·83**
All except second-year Mothers	343	+0·95*
Second-year Fathers attending	6	+15·40**
Second-year Fathers not attending	89	+3·08**
All except second-year Fathers	343	+0·95*
Any second-year Parent attending	12	+11·42**
Neither second-year Parent attending	83	+2·76**
All except second-year Parents	343	+0·95*

Mean differences marked with one asterisk were significant at the 5 per cent level; those with two asterisks at the 1 per cent level or higher.

Case studies

We know now that the children whose parents attended the reading meeting did improve, but we do not know whether

Tests of Educational Performance

this was a consequence of the meeting or indeed of anything else that happened in the school during the trial period. In order to throw a little light on this question we conducted a series of miniature case studies. For this purpose we went to 27 homes to talk to parents who had attended either the Reading or the Arithmetic meeting.

Some parents (and the same goes for teachers) gave the impression that they did not want to admit that there had been any changes in their behaviour. They were resistant, as though to admit there had been a change would be to admit there was something to criticize in their previous ways. Out of the 27 families, eight did not overtly change at all as a result of the meetings, or indeed of any other innovation made during the trial. With one of these there was no obvious reason why they should. The son was already the brightest boy in the school, and doing well in all subjects. His parents – the father a solicitor and mother a psychiatrist – were doing pretty much all that could be desired to help and encourage him. Another one was like the first in at least one way: they were themselves already assisting in almost too many ways at home. Mr. and Mrs. Turton had taught their son to write before he went to school, had read to him every night since he was two, taken him regularly to the library from the age of three, visited museums and buildings frequently, and pegged away constantly at arithmetic.

> 'We have sums about three times a week. We've gone through the lot. Times tables when they were little. Money sums. It helps them to save and count their money.'

Mr. and Mrs. Barton had also been accustomed to doing a great deal, visiting practically every museum and other places of interest in London. They thought there had been too much argument at the meeting. The fourth family was the Miltons. They had always done everything they could do to help that they felt themselves capable of but had never thought they should take a hand in Reading and Arithmetic,

Tests of Educational Performance

as they didn't consider themselves intelligent enough to grasp how these subjects were taught. The fifth family was the Johnsons. The parents didn't acknowledge that anything had changed in their home, except perhaps they felt a little more goodwill for the school. They didn't think that education was all that important for their daughter, who would get married anyway. 'Not that I want her to scrub floors and all, but be something nice, you know, like a cashier or in an office.' The last three families were Italian. None of the parents understood much of what was said at the meeting. One son told the interviewer, though, that it made a big difference to him to have his mother come to the school – he felt he had to try harder to make her feel proud of him. He had looked at all the schools programmes on the B.B.C. during the Easter holidays.

The first thing to say about the other 19 is that it was not possible in any way to isolate the influence of the meetings. The parents who said that in one way or another they had changed did not attribute this just to that. They often mentioned other features of the school, especially the private talks with the teachers.

Of the 19, twelve said they had taken to giving their child active help at home with his or her school-work.

James. (Arithmetic, up from 79 to 83. Scores relate to which meeting attended.) Had bought books recommended by the teacher, and read to Joey regularly now. His elder sister gave him sums to do as part of the game of schools they sometimes played. Games of 'school' played at home were mentioned by several parents. They seem almost as popular as games of 'home' played at school – this perhaps being some roundabout evidence of the wish of some children to join up the two halves of their lives.

Royston. (Arithmetic, up from 101 to 106.) His teacher now sent books and homework for Billy to do. The parents liked to go over it with him. Mrs. Royston felt she had more confidence about helping since the meeting, having realized that the method of arriving at the answers mattered more than the answer itself. 'The modern idea is, it doesn't matter if the answer's correct as long as the working out's all right.' Like several other parents the Roystons said how pleased their son was when they went up to the school. 'My son's tickled pink if I say I'm going up there.'

Marks. (Reading, up from 70 to 89.) Since the visits mother and son had given private 'tuition' to Milly at night. 'With pad and pen my boy and myself write different things down and she copies it.' Milly might not have got very much of value directly from this, but, according to her mother, she very much appreciated being the centre of so much interest, and, perhaps as a result, had enjoyed school much more than ever before.

Toynbee. (Arithmetic, up from 97 to 116.) Since the meeting the parents had helped their son to work out the 'new subtracting method', bought plenty of books for him, and father, who is in building trade, made a special point of picking up and passing on to son books from abandoned houses awaiting demolition. Kept Henry Miller's *Tropic of Cancer* for himself. Both parents thought the new arrangements, especially for private talks with teachers, much better than the old. 'Before, on Open Night we never got a chance to see the teacher on her own.' Though much of what was said at the meetings was above Mrs. Toynbee's head, it seemed to her she began to understand it all a bit better later on when she talked it over with some of the other mothers who had also been there, and whom she met outside the school.

Roger. (Arithmetic, up from 91 to 104.) Mr. Roger tried to help his daughter with arithmetic though not too sure he understood the method. At one point he wrote to Arabella's teacher to try and explain what her confusion was over fractions. The teacher then gave her a private lesson, which helped a lot. He said his conscience had been pricked by all the efforts being made by the school, and he felt honourbound to take more interest in his children than he had.

Crossley. (Arithmetic, down from 99 to 90.) Both parents said

Tests of Educational Performance

they had made extra efforts. Mr. Crossley was putting in extra time on arithmetic, and both of them had tried out new ways of reading. They had been to more museums and plays. 'Previously we didn't know whether helping the children at home would be regarded as interfering by the school. We were pleased to find out the opposite was true. We are willing to take any advice from the school.' Mrs. Crossley was so pleased with the school that she'd started boasting about it at her work, and irritated her work-mates with 'At John Lilburne this, at John Lilburne that'.

Joliet. (Arithmetic, up from 93 to 107; Reading, for another child, up from 98 to 125.) Both parents took a keen interest in Vincent's progress, and gave him daily reading and writing practice. 'The visits have given us confidence. We feel we can go and talk at any time.

Morris. (Arithmetic, down from 100 to 97.) Mr. Morris said he'd never understood fractions before. He claimed he now did. 'I asked Jane if she knew how to work out fractions and she didn't know either. I pointed it all out to her and she saw it clearly then.'

O'Hara. (Arithmetic, up from 94 to 96.) The parents drew upon the home for learning, for instance by letting the children weigh various ingredients for cooking on the kitchen scales. Mr. O'Hara made his son a little microscope.

Firebrace. (Reading, up from 70 to 85.) Mrs. Firebrace only realized at the meeting that she'd been trying to teach her daughter to read by a method entirely different from that of the school. No wonder she did not get on too well. 'Many other parents have had the same experience.'

Barnes. (Arithmetic, up from 94 to 96.) Both parents said they had got most out of the talk with the teacher. She had demonstrated the way arithmetic was taught, and the panrets had therefore changed their approach at home. They spoke glowingly, as many other parents had, about Mr. Pym; he had made such an effort to win them over.

Savage. (Arithmetic, up from 72 to 81.) Mrs. Savage said the meeting was 'way above my head' except that she did get the point about doing practical sums, 'like what you get in real life'. She now helped a little at home whereas she hadn't before.

The rest did not report any specific steps they had taken. Their comments were (in so far as they can be categorized at all) that they were more 'relaxed' and the like. Here is the kind of thing they said.

Jenty (Arithmetic, up from 105 to 108)
'We've learned that compared to other children he's doing very well. Before we were pressing him too much. We expected too much of him. We didn't realize he was quite average compared to other children. Now we leave him alone to work it out for himself.'

Moody (Reading, up from 82 to 84)
'We were especially pleased after going to the reading meeting to find that there were poorer readers than Danny and that he really wasn't so awful and that other parents were in the same boat as us.'

Jarman (Arithmetic, up from 125 to 136; Reading, up from 98 to 104)
'I suppose I am more relaxed about bothering the school. I know the teachers better.'

Marco (Arithmetic, up from 87 to 105)
'I think this is what I have learned from these meetings, that perhaps I have been expecting too much from my son. I do not press them to do things so much, especially as they are doing so well.'

Pilley (Reading, up from 114 to 119)
Reassured by hearing from teacher that son is one of the best in class. Thought understood teaching methods better as a result of talking about them with other mothers immediately after school meeting over.

Barkley (Reading, up from 70 to 89)
Both parents had been worried about lack of progress at reading. They used to sit down with Harry to try and teach him by the 'break-it-up' method but were rather put off by Harry's announcing that 'we don't do it like that at school'. Since the meeting they had not tried to teach themselves.

Tests of Educational Performance

Martin (Reading, down from 92 to 87)
    The meeting had not impressed Mr. and Mrs. Martin. But the teacher had, very much, and they felt that their son was in the best of hands.

Summing up

Our interpretation is bound to be tentative, since we do not have all the evidence we would have liked. There was certainly some slight though significant improvement in scores on three of the tests, most notably for arithmetic. Given a fall we could have concluded that the trial had been a failure. But the obverse does not apply. The rise does not necessarily mean that the trial was a success, however limited. It was not if 'practice effect' was responsible, and this cannot be excluded. The results for the Thorne and Fenton schools do not serve to exclude it. We suggest it probably had more influence on Non-Verbal scores than on others. To take the analysis further we isolated particular groups of parents who had, and had not, responded overtly to the various invitations. This evidence was rather hopeful – at any rate on one point. The children of parents who attended the reading meeting did do better than others. A series of miniature case studies illustrated the sort of effect the connection with the school had had on some parents. These showed that closer contact *could* produce beneficial effects for some children, even if they did not demonstrate that the overall rise was due to this cause.

We shall be on firmer ground when further trials have been made in schools of many different kinds. A great deal more intensive inquiry into the parent – child – teacher interaction is also needed. So far the school and the family have been much more studied on their own than together. Educational psychology and sociology have advanced almost as far as family psychology and sociology, but separately. The time has come to combine psychology and sociology for this task and to focus on a common subject of

Tests of Educational Performance

study, the interaction of family and school. This will mean beginning with intensive observation of individual children and following them backwards and forwards from one habitat to another, from home to school and school to home, as frequently as will be tolerated. Once more extensive *and* more intensive studies have been made it should be possible to be much less tentative than we had to be about the conclusions in this chapter.

7
CUM PARENTE

It looks as though there may be something in the 'syllogism of parental participation'.

> A rise in the level of parental encouragement augments their children's performance at school.
>
> Teachers by involving parents in the school bring about a rise in the level of parental encouragement.
>
> Teachers by involving parents in the school augment the children's performance.

But we cannot be sure. This was only a case study in one school and needs (as we have said) to be repeated before the particular can be made more general. This is especially necessary because we, the investigators, are partisan. We believe that whatever their class or income, creed or colour, parents have the right to be informed about what goes on in the school which their children attend and consulted about what should be done there. Our bias – in this context any belief is a bias – must have influenced the outcome of our research and may have led us to interpret our findings in such a way as to favour our thesis. Some of the further studies should therefore be done by people (if they can be tempted to try and demonstrate our error) who have and are willing to declare opposite, or at any rate different, biases from ours.

With these cautionary words we are for the rest of this chapter going to leave caution behind and speculate about our subject a little more generally and freely than we have done so far. There are three sections:

Cum Parente

1. The teachers' opposition;
2. Changes in the family; and
3. The emergence of a new practice.

(1) The teacher's opposition

The syllogism will not be acted upon unless teachers wish parents to participate. But do they? We were not too optimistic before this particular trial began. The Heads we had visited were (as we have said) virtually at one in their unanimity that they had 'very good relations with parents in our school'; this though they may never have set eyes on more than a minority of parents nor had any programme for involving them. The standards by which they judged what was 'very good' were evidently not ours. The same factor turned out to be critical at John Lilburne. Our first round of interviews with parents led us to think that in them was an untapped source of support for the school. It was when we arrived in the staffroom that we knew we were up against it. We were outsiders, laymen at that, and this would account for some of the reserve. But not all. There was something else. We knew then, before the trial had begun, that its success would be limited.

The attitude of teachers is so crucial that we have wondered about it a good deal, and still find it puzzling. One clue comes from some admittedly hazardous comparisons we have made between countries. Our impressions come not so much from the literature – as far as we know there have not yet been any thorough comparisons made of the role of parents in the educational systems of different countries[1] – as from visits made to schools elsewhere on behalf of the Plowden Committee. The striking impression gained from these visits was that Britain stood out in contrast not just to some but to almost all the other countries. In most of the others parents seemed, by British standards, closely associ-

---

[1] This would be an excellent subject for some post-graduate research in the universities. Study of comparative education is bound to become more and more important for sociology and psychology.

Cum Parente

ated with the school both informally and formally through every sort of Council, Committee and Association of Parents or of Parent-Teachers. More than that, parents were apparently liable to be called upon quite deliberately by the teachers to bring pressure upon the children. Here is one account, this time as it happens from a study made in France, of what happened in one school:

> 'Most parents not only insist that their children attend school regularly, but they demand of their children the best possible performance in school. If the teacher tells a family that their child is not doing as well as he might in school, that he is not working hard enough, the child's life at home becomes uncomfortable. He is constantly reminded of his deficiency. He is told that he is disgracing the family. He is deprived of play opportunities and given extra work. Every possible pressure is brought to bear on him so that he may be forced to live up to the teachers' and the parents' expectations.'[1]

The Russian system has been outlined by Mr. Grant. Every class has its parents' meeting, from which is elected the 'Parents' Trinity' to serve on the Parents' Committee of the whole school. The Parents' Committee arranges help for parents who are having difficulties with their children and its members themselves interview troublesome children, as well as supplying leaders and equipment for the extracurricular activities which are so well developed in the Soviet Union. Sometimes extreme measures may be taken.

> 'A recent case in Kiev can serve as an example; in the Krasny factory a notice was pinned up (by another parent) to the effect that Anatoly Orlenko, Class IV pupil, was behaving badly at school. Orlenko senior speedily found himself before the factory committee, and was told that he ought to do something about this, since it reflected on the factory as well as the child, the parent, and the school. . . . Techniques of this kind are effective, but rarely used; they are regarded as a drastic step to be used only when gentler methods have failed.'[2]

[1] Wylie, L., *Village in the Vaucluse*, p. 60.
[2] Grant, N., *Soviet Education*, p. 62.

Cum Parente

The same sort of thing is far from unknown even in the country whose educational system has had most influence upon ours both by way of attraction and repulsion. The common view in Britain is that in the United States with its ubiquitous P.T.A.s, which reflect the idea of the school as belonging to the local community, the situation is the other way round from that just described, in other words that there the parents control the schools. This is put forward as though it were a statement of fact, but not very convincingly since normally no evidence is adduced. It may happen, we would say it sometimes certainly does happen, but at any rate on visits paid to U.S. schools by members of the Plowden Committee, P.T.A.s were certainly always in existence – in one Negro school in the Southern States the P.T.A. member for each class was present to greet them – but it was never alleged that any of them controlled their schools. It seemed to be more common for the teachers to use P.T.A.s as a means of influencing the parents.

Making use of parents as an instrument of school policy is bound to seem distasteful to people brought up in the English tradition – it sometimes does to us. One also has to admit that, distasteful or not, these methods could be highly effective,[1] and their use in other countries and their absence in Britain may both account for, and reflect, differences in popular attitudes to education. The failure to find a style of parental co-operation that would be acceptable in Britain may account in part for the singular lack of support for scholarship and the school in many working-class homes. There is a great difference between say the French conception of '*le bon élève*' and the English conception of 'the swot', and if the lack of co-operation between school and home accounts in some degree for the difference it also accounts

[1] Children are quite capable of seeing that a combination of home and school could be an uncomfortably strong one. One mother at John Lilburne said, 'Jimmy is like a lot of youngsters – their Mum mustn't go with him up to the school. If he's done something a little bit wrong then he won't entertain me going up there. "Oh no, Mum," he says, "there's no need to go round." He'll sort it out, himself, he says.'

Cum Parente

for the most serious weakness there is in British education.

If Britain was the odd country out only as far as parents are concerned, and that was all there was to it, one could perhaps be reasonably optimistic that foreign example could, and even perhaps would, be followed once it became recognized that in this respect other countries had an asset of which we were depriving ourselves. But it is not so simple as that. The relative lack of parental co-operation – a disadvantage for Britain – seems to be linked with two advantages the country has – the tradition of pastoral care and the autonomy of the teacher. If we are right in our analysis the question is whether the link between the two pluses and the one minus can be broken.

The tradition of pastoral care stems in part from the private boarding schools which are of such unique historical as well as contemporary importance in Britain. They have in all sorts of ways set the norms for the rest to follow. In them the teachers have to act as parents. But in day schools as well as boarding the teachers are also considered to be *in loco parentis* instead of *cum parente*, responsible for inculcating moral standards as well as instruction, for giving encouragement to their children and also for disciplining them. It is no accident that in almost all other countries corporal punishment in schools (and sometimes at home too) is illegal or frowned on. They do not need corporal punishment because they have the parents whereas in Britain with its corporal punishment teachers probably have to face more severe problems in maintaining control in the classroom than almost anywhere. Young teachers in particular are sometimes quite obsessed with the problems of discipline, especially in schools like John Lilburne. Elsewhere corporal punishment along with much other discipline is work for parents, not teachers, which is one reason why the latter must communicate with the former so as to be able to invoke their authority when necessary. In Britain the teacher who was as much the instructor pure as his counterpart in some other countries, who would take no part in the ceremonies

Cum Parente

of school meals and playground, who always whipped home when the last bell rang, would not be thought the complete teacher by any of the heirs to the Arnold tradition.

The British ideal is of the surrogate parent, and if one is setting oneself up as that, the presence of the real parent may be nothing but an embarrassment. But the ideal, though it prevents a sterile isolation of intellectual from emotional and physical development[1] and though it can nourish the most praiseworthy dedication, has seldom fitted as well in the day schools of the Bethnal Greens of this century as it did in the Rugbys of the last; and indeed as it still does in many present-day boarding schools and in a different way in some of the first-class secondary schools where the school-day for neither staff nor pupil finishes when lessons stop. Certainly we should keep what is good about pastoral care. But does it follow that parents must be excluded just because one has a larger conception of one's functions than as an instructor? The tradition could surely be preserved in general without that bit of it, and teachers keep a wide-ranging responsibility which was nevertheless shared rather than exclusive, *cum parente* rather than *in loco parentis*.

The autonomy of the classroom

Autonomy raises still more difficult questions. Once again it appears that Britain is the odd country out: in what they shall teach in and out of the classroom, and how they shall do it, teachers are allowed more freedom than elsewhere. The influence of the private schools which preceded the State establishment has again been dominant. One cannot even talk as in so many things of an Anglo-Saxon tradition extending beyond the island; in America the State Governments and the School Boards, in other Commonwealth

---

[1] The Hadow Report defined the attitude at its best when it said that 'our main care must be to supply children between the ages of 7 and 11 with what is essential to their healthy growth – physical, intellectual, and moral – during that particular stage of their development'. *Report of the Consultative Committee on the Primary School.* 1931, p. 74.

Cum Parente

countries the State or Provincial governments lay down from outside the school what the curriculum shall be inside it in a way that would be unthinkable in Britain (or at any rate has never been proposed since Payment by Results was abolished). Across the Atlantic and the Pacific the government carries almost as much authority in the educational domain as it does in the Common Market countries. The difference is not, of course, as great as the formal structure suggests. The edicts of Moscow or Paris, Albany or Sacramento are interpreted by good teachers in a flexible way, which makes them more like us, and to make us more like them, in secondary schools in Britain external examiners, who even if they are themselves teachers are at least outside the individual school, have gained a stranglehold on the curriculum which teachers seem loth to break even when they are offered the opportunity, as they have been with the externally moderated C.S.E.

The difference still remains, in attitude as well as in practice. Most American and Russian observers, however charitable, would hardly find a good word to say about autonomy at a school like John Lilburne if it means that there is not even a common plan within the school (let alone including the Infants) about the methods to be used by different members of the staff for teaching reading or any other subject; and would rejoice in their happier state where prescription from outside, complete with standard timetable and standard primers, does at least provide on paper for a common plan of working. Most British observers, and we with them, would accept the force of such criticism but still believe that on balance this country has the best of it. Prescription of the curriculum by the State is apt to leave the teacher as an instrument for conveying standardized knowledge. It can harden the division between 'subjects', arithmetic, geography, history and so forth, which look so neat in separate boxes on a timetable but are often so much better combined. It can detract from spontaneity and remove the need for each teacher to determine how and what to try and

Cum Parente

teach with his own particular skills to the particular children in front of or around him. Autonomy produces some of the worst teaching in the Western world but at the same time it produces some of the best, as shown to great advantage in the primary schools. We would not easily be persuaded that the average is not higher than elsewhere.

Most teachers would not perhaps argue for autonomy on quite these grounds. They would put much more stress on the need for teachers to have a professional status as high and as secure as that of doctors, lawyers and the rest. The mark of a profession is that its members are free to make their own expert and independent judgements about what is in the best interests of their 'clients' – be they patients, litigants or pupils. But they must be expert, and this means restricting the role to those with specialized qualifications and experience. Whatever the argument, it leads to the same conclusion. The encroachment of outsiders must be prevented, auxiliaries kept out of the classroom[1] and along with them (many would say) the parents.

It is not easy to pick one's way through these issues. We have argued that the defensiveness against parents which we are strongly against has belonged with a style of academic freedom which we are as strongly for. But we ask again whether the one must necessarily go with the other. To accept parents as partners would not necessarily derogate from the professionalism of teachers. They would still have their sphere in which educational questions were decided by them alone in the end, even though they took the trouble to inform parents of their decisions. But in a sense the sphere of their professionalism would have been enlarged: they would (to anticipate a later section) need to become more expert, not less, if they were going to engage parents on behalf of their children's education. If they did so successfully they would have found allies not just for the children but for themselves.

[1] For a discussion of the drive for professional status see Musgrave, P. W., *The Sociology of Education*, Chapter 13, and Tropp, A., *The Teachers*.

Cum Parente

(2) Changes in the family

The tense was subjunctive. We are not there yet by a long way, and the pace of progress will not depend so much upon the strength of an argument, let alone on the results of research, as upon the degree to which the underlying dispositions of parents and teachers are altering. We talked about teachers in the last section. In this we are more concerned with parents. Perhaps the most obvious change affecting them is simply that more middle-class people of a kind who a half-century ago would have sent their children to private schools are now sending them to maintained ones instead. Many of them do not need very much convincing about the message of this book – they know that encouragement makes a great deal of difference to their children, and they know too that to make it fully effective they need to understand what goes on at school. The arrival on the educational scene in the last few years of the consumer of education represented by new organizations like the Advisory Centre for Education (A.C.E.) and the Confederation for the Advancement of State Education (C.A.S.E.), and the setting up in the autumn of 1967 of the Home and School Council by these two organizations along with the National Federation of Parent-Teacher Associations, are only symptoms of this change in the class composition of children at State schools. We would say the same about the issue from Curzon Street of the first publication there has ever been purely on the subject of parents.

The views of this minority of middle-class parents have not so far been shared in general by the great majority, rather the opposite. Working-class people have not been nearly so anxious to get into the school. The class barrier has something to do with it – the difficulty which people from different levels have in communicating without embarrassment. This is particularly sharp when parents and teachers live in different places and cannot get to know each other outside the school – indeed all that we are saying in this book

Cum Parente

applies much more to big cities than to towns and villages. But as well as that, parent-teacher non-association has been supported by the respect which many manual workers feel for job boundaries. They expect that in their own work demarcation rules should be observed, and they are prepared to be consistent about it when it comes to others. In the course of this inquiry we heard many people and had heard many more before say that the teacher must be left to get on with his job:

> 'What I say is a teacher is a teacher and doesn't come into the parents' interests at all. As regards schools – it's school. We don't know how to teach. Can't go to a teacher and say you're not teaching my son correctly. It's like somebody coming home and telling me my job.'

> 'The trouble is that people today are so education-conscious. It's a bit overdone. I'd put it like this. If anyone tried to teach me my job I would soon tell them where to go. And teaching is their job, not ours.'

Most teachers would probably not be as charitable as this about demarcation rules in industry. But there is some reciprocal sympathy all the same. Along with that well-worn one about America, a stock argument used by teachers against the formation of P.T.A.s in their schools – it is still only a few Heads who have not only tolerated them but shown how useful they can be as a link between school and home – is that, falling into the hands of the middle-class, they will make other parents feel excluded and inferior. The argument clearly has some force to it and would have more if the Head were not able to use his/her undoubted influence to prevent such an outcome.

Changing structure of the family

The reasons for it are no doubt debatable; but the fact that non-association has been pretty stable throughout most of the first century of compulsory education can hardly be denied. Why then do we believe that a change is on the way?

Cum Parente

To say why means going back a little into history, and summarizing some previous Institute reports. The proposition advanced there was that the families of the poor suffered most from the Industrial Revolution, and have correspondingly recovered most in the last quarter of a century. Amongst the poor the family had held together in agriculture and domestic handicraft because it was the unit of production just as the better-off families had been sustained by their possession of family property. When the economic tie went the whole structure was threatened. At the time of the Booth survey at the end of the last century the whole had almost broken up into its parts. The man, in particular, was often an absentee husband and an absentee father spending on himself what should have gone on his wife and children. This long decline has now been stopped and a degree of family unity restored. Invention has brought functions back even to relatively poor homes – television has replaced the cinema and much other outside entertainment and quite far down the income scale the motor car has added to the home a mobile room in which the husband can carry his wife about (as yet the working-class wife seldom drives herself) and the children too. Do-it-yourself has also revived 'cottage industries' of a sort. More money has made the home comfortable enough to keep the man out of the pub and more leisure has given him more time and more energy to spend with his wife and children. It is hardly surprising that marriage is more popular than it ever was with teachers as well as everyone else – and that the size of family has for a period been edging upwards after over fifty years of decline.

Educational functions were at first lost along with the rest. Before the coming of industry, in their self-contained communities where the soil was widely distributed among peasant holders and all articles of common necessity and convenience were supplied by the joint labour of the family, the family itself had been the only forum of instruction.[1] So it

[1] Dobbs, A. E., *Education and Social Movements, 1700–1850*.

Cum Parente

has to some extent remained for mothers and their daughters since they inherit the same principal jobs. But for men there has been a great change. When the fathers were employed in industry and particularly when their sons did not follow them in the same occupation, they had much less to teach them. The main responsibility for instructing their sons (and of course to a large extent their daughters too) was transferred from the home to the school and transferred rather completely, as we have seen, with the parents contracting out, as well as being forced out, of any stake at all in the school.

We are sure that the situation is changing again, as the family, for educational purposes, follows the same spiral of development as it has in general, from supremacy through decline to recovery. Parents are increasingly recognizing that their children can better themselves in occupational terms if they take advantage of their educational opportunities and that they, as parents, may be able to improve their children's chances. Manual workers have been the last to give up a belief in an exclusive genetic determination of ability, which was less wounding to self-respect than it would have been to accept that they were where they were (with no chance of betterment) because of a failure of effort. But they are giving it up now, with television as one of the catalysts. To Mrs. Finch, an informant on this inquiry, the historical transition was compressed in between one end and another of a paragraph. In one breath she said:

> 'I think if a child has it in her, if she has the ability she will get on. I don't believe you should force them.'

In the next she veered around –

> 'Did you hear that talk on the tellie by them professors. Only last week it was. They said it was not your ability that counts but the way you're made to do it and the help you get. And I think they're right.'

Mrs. Finch was almost ready to start reading to her daughter

Cum Parente

at night; and with her go the many other mothers and fathers who would now welcome a partnership. It will not be long before they are demanding it, and at that point the old formal non-intervention agreement between teachers and manual workers will be dead.

(3) *The emergence of a new practice*

Earlier on we said that the French or the Russian practice had its disadvantages. Their mobilization of the home to shame children into diligence seems almost as cruel to us as our use of corporal punishment would to them. But if not that, what is to be done? At this stage no one can be too sure. A new tradition has to be created, since for once, although outstanding pioneering work has already been done in some schools,[1] there is as yet no firm indigenous one on which to lean. A new tradition will not come quickly. Energetic teachers who believe that parents can be an educational force will devise (probably already have devised) far better measures than we have thought of. Yet we cannot finish without saying something beyond what has already been proposed in the Plowden Report and by the Ministry about what in our view might be done.

As far as formalities go we would not depart so very far from what was done at John Lilburne, especially after the first six months' trial when Mr. Pym was on his own. Pride of place would, if we were starting again, still be given to the private talks with teachers. But we would suggest that as well as an appointment being made for this purpose early in each school year (never at the end when parent and child are just about to be passed on to another teacher), all teachers should also be asked to stay behind for a few hours in their classrooms for a monthly 'surgery' when they would be available for consultation in the afternoons by any parent who wanted to see them and was free to come then. Occasionally

---

[1] Mr. McGeeney is producing a report on good practice in parent-teacher relations called *Parents are Welcome* which should be published soon after this.

Cum Parente

these would be in the evenings for the convenience of fathers as well as working mothers. Likewise, the Head would set aside a period each week when he could be seen without appointment by any parent. In addition, all parents would be told that they would be welcome (if there was room for them) to attend School Assembly on a particular, or even every, morning of the week, and afterwards to look around the classrooms. Opportunity would also be given for parents to learn about the teaching methods of the school. These and other formal arrangements would be described in a regular circular letter sent out at least once a term. A P.T.A. or similar organization would be set up if only to symbolize the fact that a new phase had been entered: that now parents as well as teachers had a measure of joint responsibility for the school.

The real problem comes not in drawing up such a list but in knowing how best to conduct the various functions, for instance, the meetings about teaching methods which we have just advocated again, despite all the trouble we had at John Lilburne. The reasons we do so are not difficult to summarize. Few parents will sit by if they see their child in need of help over some blockage that has developed in the process of learning. At the secondary stage they have often got to, because the child has already passed beyond them in knowledge. At the primary stage they have a choice. They usually know how to do the 3Rs and will think they may be able to assist, especially over the 'reading crisis' which may easily embroil the whole family whenever a child is thought to be slow in mastering the skill which is, even in an age of television, essential. If this be accepted, the question for the teacher is whether or not to try and teach the parent enough to enable him to answer the child's questions or to show him how to find out the answer for himself. Wherever there has been a change in technique since the parent was at school, and increasingly there has and is going to be, the alternative is only too liable to be muddle for the child. If our inquiry has shown anything it is the uncertainty aroused in many parents' minds by this very advance. Unless the parents know how things are done now, they are likely to sow their own confusion in the minds of their children.

Learning by discovery

Yet how difficult it is in practice to remove it. Many parents are not capable of comprehending anything from pamphlets (these were one of the more obvious failures at John Lilburne) or from formal talks delivered, as if at an adult education class, from a top table. They will only learn if they take an active part of some kind, for instance by trying out and discovering the purpose of various pieces of classroom apparatus for themselves instead of being told about them. The activity methods for which primary schools are famous are not only suitable for children. Parents should also have the chance to talk rather than be talked at. Then fewer parents would say as one of our informants said about teachers in general – 'With teachers you cannot get a word in edgeways.' If they are given the chance to open their mouths some new ideas may jump in. They may be led to formulate some questions for themselves and if they do they may remember the answers when they get them. The teacher is more likely, for most of the time, to achieve some result by listening than by talking himself.

Parents are most likely of all to learn in association with the person they really care about in the school, their own child. Much of the very best teaching washes over into the home anyway – the child is so excited by it that he involves his father and mother willy-nilly. This we would see as one of the most hopeful models of all. The more teachers can encourage parents and children to learn together, the more they are likely to strengthen each other's interest. The national survey made for the Plowden Committee showed that most parents would like their children to be given homework. And why not? Homework need not mean what it has often meant in the past – dull cramming exercises.

Cum Parente

There could be a new sort of 'homework' mainly designed to involve parents in learning with their children. Some schools have, for example, achieved good results by asking children expressly with the help of their parents to work out the cost of the paint needed to redecorate the kitchen at home, to conduct a mini traffic census in their street, to make costumes for a school play and to reconstruct the recent history of their district by collecting for an exhibition in the school old photographs and other objects which show how people used to live. And if parents are asked to help the school by constructing gardens, swimming pools, shelves and stages, and even additional classrooms or a parents' clubroom to go in the playground, their children should be associated with them as far as possible. Where this sort of thing has been done a gain greater than the constructions (useful though these can be) has been the pride of the fathers, and of their children in them, when in the setting of the school they can for once excel by the display of some skills they possess in greater measure than the teachers.

However advanced the programme it will never be fully effective if the object is seen only as the enlightenment of the parents. It is just as important that the teachers should be enlightened in their turn. Ideally, parents should take part in working out the programme of action for each year, and asked to put forward any suggestions they have about ways of improving the organization of the school. To begin with, parents accustomed to a different régime might have little to say. But nearly always they are more knowledgeable at any rate on one vital matter – their own child – than the teacher, and they should have every opportunity to tell him what they know. This can be done in a general way by following Mr. Pym[1] and asking the parents to send him a regular 'report' on their children, and less formally in the talks with him and with teachers.

[1] On this he was acting on the precedent of what Mr. Green had done in another primary school. See Green, L., *Parents and Teachers – Partners or Rivals?*

Cum Parente

The absentee parents

In all this we have had in mind the parents who are ready for a partnership of varying degrees of closeness. But not all the Mrs. Finches are like that, as we have seen. What then is to be done about the parents who will not respond to any invitation? This has been a subsidiary theme of the book. We hoped that the teachers at John Lilburne would visit most of such parents in their own homes. The teachers were not willing. Even if they had been, we are now doubtful whether we were right to hope they would. Several of these parents, and grandparents, had their own reasons for not going to the school. They had mostly suffered misfortune. We are not saying this is the only reason for non-attendance – far from it. But amongst non-attenders there would probably always be a high proportion of parents who kept clear of the school because they were sufficiently embarrassed by their circumstances not to want the teachers to know about them. Even where the parents were agreeable, it does not necessarily follow that a home visit would be in the interests of the child. A child may want, as we said, to keep the two halves of his life separate, and find a refuge in each from the other. Too close a connection between parents and teachers could seem to the child like a ganging up of adults against him.

Should the parents who cannot be persuaded to come to the school then be left entirely to themselves? We think that would be going too far in the opposite direction. As a general rule a child's class teacher is not perhaps the right person. But there should be someone who does visit, a third party who yet knows a good deal about the school and can through practice build up special skills in home interviewing. Not all parents would be seen, of course, only those who agreed to a visit. But if our experience is any guide there would be quite enough consenting parents to give such a third party plenty to do.

It would be worthwhile for several reasons.[1] Sometimes

---
[1] As shown by Mays, J. B., in *Education and the Urban Child*.

Cum Parente

the parents who do not take anything in from a written communication could be shown that a visit by them to the school of their own free will would be of value to the child. Sometimes anxieties about the child could be removed. Sometimes a misunderstanding could be removed, of the kind illustrated in Chapter 5. Sometimes the parents, if it were acceptable to them, could be put in touch with other social services which might be able to give them support, and the attention of other professional social workers drawn to needs of families that might otherwise be overlooked. They should have priority over other claimants on social workers if only because they have young children in them.

If no other function was served, such visits would at least help a little to remove the suspicion of 'them' harboured by many people who have suffered misfortune. The outside world, which includes the school, is liable to seem threatening partly because it is all so impersonal. Once the school is represented not by forms, not by circular letters, not by the outside of a forbidding building but by a person, it would be visualized in a rather different light. The need for this new kind of social worker has been accepted in Glasgow, Oxfordshire and some other places. The Director of Education for Oxfordshire has said that 'about 30 per cent to 40 per cent of parents do not attend school functions; in these and other cases correspondence is time-taking and ineffective. The only successful way is through personal link and contact for which the majority of teachers have not the time, and they are often not the best fitted for the work'.[1]

We too are asking for a third party, and this implies that attached to every school, particularly those which have many immigrant children, should be an education social worker, perhaps better called an 'Education Visitor',[2] to point the parallel with Health Visitors. His or her main job,

[1] Chorlton, A. R., 'Attaching Social Workers to Schools' in Craft, M. Raynor, J., and Cohen, L., *Linking Home and School*, p. 184.
[2] Young, M., 'Parent-Teacher Co-operation', in *Linking Home and School*, ibid.

Cum Parente

apart from helping to organize the kind of parents' activities described in Chapter 4, would be to maintain communication with the parents who stay away from them. Many of the present Educational Welfare Officers (though their names would be changed to Education Visitors) could be specially trained for the work, partly by being given the chance to learn about what happens inside the schools outside which they are going to spend much of their time.

Though a third party would in our view do the job best, partly because he or she was not directly responsible for the child in question, we would obviously not want to rule out other people, particularly teachers who were also social workers. Such people are as yet only being trained in tiny numbers, for instance by the Edge Hill College of Education. But in any school which could spare a suitable member of staff, through heads taking classes and by other expedients, he or she could work either mornings or afternoons in the classroom and evenings or week-ends in the neighbourhood both visiting and helping to organize activities for parents in the evenings. If the person were given a special responsibility allowance for parent-teacher relations that would at least mark the importance of the work. There should also be experiments with volunteer Education Visitors, who could be drawn from parents as well as others, their object being the same as that underlying all the other suggestions we have made, the creation of a partnership between school and home.

The exchange of information

Whatever is done, it is important that there should be as full an exchange of information as possible about the devices for enlisting parental interest that are tried in one school or another. The autonomy of which we have spoken several times means that there is throughout the country a remarkable variety of practice in every feature of school organization, arrangements for parents along with the rest. But

Cum Parente

teachers do not get anything like full value for the variety. Despite the fine work of the H.M.I.s and despite the educational journals, so often they do not know anything about other schools, even those in the same neighbourhood. We hope that as far as dealings with parents are concerned this will be less true in the future than it has been in general in the past.

Research will also be needed in order to provide the checks which teachers cannot draw from their own unaided common sense. The study reported in this book is an example – common sense could not tell us whether efforts to involve parents would be for the benefit of their children's educational performance. Research cannot tell us easily either, as the last chapter showed. But it is still worth making the attempt to trace connections which go beyond the obvious, and, as we said at the beginning of this chapter, we very much hope that the kind of investigation we have made will be repeated. The rises in test scores at John Lilburne are a yardstick against which other schools can show what they can do. We hope that many of the further inquiries will be made by teachers rather than by researchers, although they should be able to draw on professional advice if they need it.

Burt advocated a co-operative scheme of research into methods of dealing with backward children as long ago as 1937. What he said applies as well today and to our field of interest.

> 'The time has certainly come for some co-operative scheme for research into the innumerable questions that arise. A single investigator can do little, except make a few limited and tentative experiments, and sketch what appear to be the most valid methods of inquiry. The teacher, the medical officer, the social worker, the psychologist, the inspector and the statistician – all need to lend their expert knowledge; but each can deal only with one limited aspect . . . Individual enterprise, uncoordinated, sporadic, can do no more than first break the ground. . . . Whatever plans are achieved in this direction might

Cum Parente

well be collected and collated, the efforts extended on some systematic plan, and the knowledge gained by each placed at the disposal of all.'[1]

Taking our cue from this plea we therefore propose to start the kind of club envisaged by Burt. It will be called 'The Home and School Research Association'. The admirable Surrey Educational Research Association has shown what can be done to sustain the inquiries of teachers organized by locality. We want to see what can be done by teachers, wherever they are, who are interested in a particular subject of research and experiment. We therefore invite any teacher, or parent, who has read so far in this book and who wishes to do research on parental participation as it affects any sort of school (not just primary schools) to write to one of the authors, i.e.

> Patrick McGeeney,
> Institute of Community Studies,
> 18, Victoria Park Square,
> London, E.2.

Limiting himself to the end of 1970 so that he does not go on getting letters into the indefinite future, he will be ready to offer suggestions about the components of action programmes and about ways of measuring their effects. We would welcome it if similar 'clubs' were formed by researchers and teachers who agree with us only about a 'cooperative scheme', not about the value of parental cooperation. We hope that the mere fact of a welcome from us will not cause our opponents to desist.

We would sum up all that we have been trying to say in some such way as this. Parents naturally want to know what is going on in this other building to which their children are now attached, what they are now expected to be good at, and how their child is faring compared to others. Their characteristic state – in this respect we would not think John Lilburne exceptional – is that of both wanting information

[1] Burt, C., *The Backward Child*, p. 625.

Cum Parente

and of not being able to get it, except in a corrupted form. It is a combination well calculated to arouse anxiety. They have to make do with such little bits of 'information' as they can get. One source is other parents. Some of them meet informally each afternoon by the gates of infant or junior schools while they wait for their children to emerge. The chief message always on the agenda of those meetings, held out of doors in all weathers, on the pavement or in the playground instead of inside the building, is that the school authorities regard them as outsiders. But uninformed as they are, the mothers share the second and third-hand snippets they have about the goings on behind the walls above them. The main source, though, is the children. They are unreliable informants. They may not understand what is happening; they may not be able to articulate it; they may deliberately mislead; or they may fail to give the information they have because they think it would be discreditable to them. In this last category children who are doing particularly badly may want to keep home and school apart so that their parents do not share the poor opinion which they know or fear their teachers have formed of them.

However much they are kept in ignorance, parents still cannot refrain from assessing their children by whatever criteria they can seize on. All have some grasp of how to judge proficiency in reading even if not of the standards which the teachers are hoping to achieve at different ages, or of the methods being used. Likewise with parrot-skill at the arithmetic tables, with spelling or neatness. 'What a neat book' a parent will say on Open Day, as though neatness was the summit of virtue. It is as if the parents were in a sort of maze in which they know that an examination is going on but since they are not told either questions or answers they have to invent their own. They are only too likely, particularly if they are liable to anxiety anyway, either to withdraw interest from something so puzzling (which means that the child may get no further support from the home for his attempts to learn) or to come to the conclusion that their

Cum Parente

children are not doing well and set expectations well beyond what is immediately possible for them to achieve. If this happens the child, motivated as we have been saying from his home environment, may develop a block which prevents progress at reading, arithmetic or whatever it may be. Uneducated parents seem to be liable to apply their own adult standards without making much allowance for age, and to become disappointed because their children seem to be so slow in acquiring the skills, say, of reading, which they themselves have.

The kind of picture we have at any rate got from our case study is of parents who are largely ignorant about the school. But if they do not contract out, they are likely to invent a kind of parody of what is actually happening in the school, devising their own independent standards of achievement and their own independent sets of expectation about the levels which the child should have reached. The result can hardly be a happy one for him. He can hardly avoid being confused by the dual values of home and school. He may react like the parents who do not cling to any educational standards, however archaic, and withdraw his interest from education altogether, or more frequently decide to do just the minimum which will ensure that with a little luck he gets by without being troubled too much by any adults. The remedy is surely for teachers to endeavour to keep parents informed about the goals which the school is trying to reach, about the techniques being used to reach them and about the standard which the child has reached. We would stress the word 'endeavour', because for a transference of information there have to be two parties, and even though the teachers were ready to give it does not follow that the parents would be ready to receive. They have had a double experience of secrecy at school, when they were at one and now that their children are, and being bred to an old régime cannot easily accept a new. It means changing a tradition.

We know that we are asking for a great deal from teachers.

Cum Parente

Many of them are already overtaxed, trying as they are to cope with too many children in classes that are too large in buildings that are decidedly not handsome and commodious. On top of this, to urge them to take on responsibility for the parents as well may seem like asking for the impossible. We only do so because we believe that it would be so much in the interests of the children, in and out of Educational Priority Areas. The lack of full co-operation with parents is one of the greatest failings of our educational system. The teachers who decide to build a new partnership will be completing the triangle of child, parent and teacher; they will be recognizing that about a particular child the parents may be in some ways more expert than they; they will be sensitive to the constant interplay of influence between home and school upon the child's capacity for life. They will be the new professionals.

APPENDIX 1

PSYCHOMETRIC TESTING

by D. N. Turland

Considerations Affecting the Selection of Tests

In order to obtain as complete an assessment of each child's potential and school performance as possible the following sorts of tests were considered appropriate:

1. A test of verbal intelligence.
2. A test of non-verbal intelligence.
3. A test of reading attainment.
4. A test of arithmetic attainment.

The nature and scope of the study imposed considerable restrictions on the choice of specific tests. Tests were finally selected with reference to the following criteria:

(*a*) adequate standardization of the tests and relevance of normative data to the particular sample;
(*b*) suitability of the tests for administration on a group basis and, where possible, by teachers;
(*c*) suitability of the tests for retesting after about six months (e.g. provision of alternative forms);
(*d*) suitability for application over the complete age range present in a Junior School.

This last requirement presented a particularly difficult problem which could not be overcome in the case of the non-verbal test where different tests were required for those children respectively above and below 8 years. Also, different tests of arithmetic attainment relevant to the stage of teaching at each year level had to be administered. In so far as standardized scores give a measure of each child's

Psychometric Testing

attainment relative to their classmates in the arithmetical operations *appropriate to their age*, this procedure was considered justified.

Description of Tests

1. *Verbal Intelligence*

   Name: The Essential Junior Intelligence Test (Form A) by Schonell and Adams; published by Oliver and Boyd.
   Retest: Form B.
   Reliability: Form A (i) Split-half method: 0·92 (N = 66).
   (ii) Test-retest after 12 months: 0·92.
   Form B   Test retest after three months: 0·92.
   Forms A and B were found to intercorrelate to the extent of 0·95 (N = 225).
   Standardization: Since different tests were used, a word should be said about the standardization. Form A was standardized with 3,200 pupils and Form B with 7,759 pupils. According to the Manual, 'careful consideration' was given to the 'groups chosen' and 'similar methods' were used for the two forms.
   Type of Score: Raw scores were converted to Mental Age equivalents from which I.Q. scores were calculated. On standardization, the distribution of Intelligence Quotients was found to follow the normal curve 'very closely' with a mean of about 103 and a standard deviation of about 16.

2. *Non-Verbal Intelligence*

   (a) Children below age 8·0
   Name: Picture Test 1, by J. E. Stuart: published by N.F.E.R.
   Retest: The same test was reapplied, there being no suitable alternative form.

Psychometric Testing

Reliability: 0·92 by Kuder-Richardson Formula 20 (N = 200).

(*b*) Children over age 8·0
Name: Non-Verbal Test 5, by D. A. Pidgeon: published by N.F.E.R.
Retest: The same test was reapplied, there being no suitable alternative form.
Reliability: 0·966 by Kuder-Richardson Formula 20 (N = 184).
Both the above tests yield standardized scores with a mean of 100 and a standard deviation of 15.

3. *Reading Attainment*

Name: Sentence Reading Test 1, by A. F. Watts: published by N.F.E.R.
Retest: The same test was reapplied there being no suitable alternative form.
Reliability: An average co-efficient of 0·94 is reported (test-retest, one week interval: N = 243).
A standardized score, mean = 100, standard deviation = 15, is obtained.

4. *Arithmetic Attainment*

(*a*) First-Year Children
Name: Mechanical Arithmetic Test 2A (N.F.E.R.).
Retest: Mechanical Arithmetic Test 2B (N.F.E.R.).
(*b*) Second-Year Children
Name: Mechanical Arithmetic Test 1A (N.F.E.R.).
Retest: Mechanical Arithmetic Test 1B (N.F.E.R.).
(*c*) Third-Year Children
Name: Arithmetic Progress Test B1 (N.F.E.R.).
Retest: Arithmetic Progress Test B2 (N.F.E.R.).
(*d*) Fourth-Year Children
Name: Arithmetic Progress Test C1 (N.F.E.R.).

Psychometric Testing

Retest: It was planned to use Test C_2; information received from the N.F.E.R. Test Services, however, indicated that this test now cannot be considered equivalent to C_1. Accordingly, Test C_1 was reapplied at retest.

The quoted reliability coefficients for the above tests are at least 0·94. All the tests yield standardized scores with a mean of 100 and a standard deviation of 15.

Standardization: For the First-, Second-, and Third-Year tests, the alternative forms were administered, on the same occasion, to children sitting in alternate rows (in an unspecified number of classrooms) in an attempt to achieve random samples for each form: equivalence was confirmed by the resulting statistical comparisons.

The total numbers participating in such studies were:

Tests 2A and 2B : 7859.
Tests 1A and 1B : 5158.
Tests B1 and B2 : 8945.

The total standardization samples were, in some cases, greatly enlarged subsequently.

Note on Validity

With reference to the Essential Intelligence Test, both the test-content and the reported correlation of 0·89 with the Terman Merrill Test can be regarded as evidence that the test is highly relevant to what psychologists usually mean by intelligence.

While such direct evidence is not available for Non-Verbal Test 5 its formal qualities were regarded as being suitable to provide useful additional information concerning a child's reasoning abilities.

The reading and arithmetic attainment tests possess validity of content for a wide range of the activities carried out in the classroom.

Psychometric Testing

Conditions of Testing

The initial testing was carried out within the period September 24th to October 13th, 1965, and the retesting within the period April 26th to May 9th, 1966.

Testing was on a group basis, according to the usual class structure. The class teacher administered the reading and arithmetic tests, following the instructions in the test manuals, and after preliminary discussion with the psychologist. The class teacher was also in charge of the Verbal Intelligence Test administration for the third- and fourth-year classes; for the first- and second-year children, the classes were divided in half during this test, half being supervised by the class teacher and the remainder by the psychologist (this procedure was adopted in order to facilitate supervision of the younger children). Non-Verbal Test 5 and Picture Test 1 were administered by the psychologist, with the assistance of the class teachers.

Care was taken to ensure that in general no child took more than one test on a given day. Absentees from the class testings – about 10 per cent of the sample – were tested later in small groups.

The second retest was carried out in the period November 7th to 18th, 1966; that is, 13 months after initial testing and 7 months after the first retest.

The complete testing programme was as follows:

	Initial Testing (Sept. 1965)	First Retest (April 1966)	Second Retest (Nov. 1966)
Verbal Intelligence Test: Essential Intelligence Test:	Form A	Form B	Form A
Non-Verbal Intelligence Test:			
(a) Children below 8·0 yrs.:	Picture Test 1 was used throughout		

Psychometric Testing

(*b*) Children above
 8·0 yrs.: Non-Verbal Test 5 was used throughout
Reading Attainment Test: Sentence Reading Test 1 was used throughout

Arithmetic Attainment Test:

1st-Year Classes:	Mechanical Arith. 2A	Mechanical Arith. 2B	Mechanical Arith. 2A
2nd-Year Classes:	Mechanical Arith. 1A	Mechanical Arith. 1B	Mechanical Arith. 1A
3rd-Year Classes:	Arithmetic Progress B1	Arithmetic Progress B2	Arithmetic Progress B1
4th-Year Classes:	Arithmetic Progress Test C1 was used throughout		

Appendix 2

QUESTIONNAIRE FOR INTERVIEWS

Serial No. | | | |

1. Can you tell me how long you have been living in this neighbourhood?
    Less than a year 1
    1 year ∠ 2 years 2
    2 years ∠ 5 years 3
    5 years ∠ 10 years 4
    10 years ∠ 15 years 5
    15 years ∠ 20 years 6
    20 years or more 7

2. Where were you born? And your husband?

	Wife	Husband
Local (within 15 mins. walk of John Lilburne)	1	1
Other London	2	2
Rest England and Wales	3	3
Scotland	4	4
Ireland	5	5
Overseas (state country)	6	6

Now can we talk about —— (SUBJECT)?

Can you give me a few details about the people in this household? How many children are there? (pre-school and school)——
Can we start with the youngest?

	Name	Relationship to informant	Sex M F	Age (in yrs)	Name of school	OFF USE
A			1 2			
B			1 2			
C			1 2			
D			1 2			
E			1 2			
F			1 2			
G			1 2			
H			1 2			

SUBJECT IS——(GIVE LETTER)

Questionnaire for Interviews

4. Now the adults. How many are there?
CHECK So there are —— of you altogether?

	Name	Relationship to informant	Sex M F	Age group 15-24 25-34 35-44 45-54 55-64 65+
I		INFORMANT	1 2	3 4 5 6 7 8
J			1 2	3 4 5 6 7 8
K			1 2	3 4 5 6 7 8
L			1 2	3 4 5 6 7 8
M			1 2	3 4 5 6 7 8

5. Did —— go to John Lilburne Infants?
    Yes 1
    No 2
IF YES (1) (a) How long was he/she there?
    —— yrs
(b) Did he/she go to any other Infant School?
    Yes 3
    No 4
(b) Why did you move him/her to John Lilburne?
IF NO (2) Which Infant School did he/she go to?
Any others?

6. Did you have a talk with his/her Infants Head when —— started at his/her first Infants School?
    Yes 5
    No 6
IF YES (5) What did you talk about?
IF NO (6) Why not?

7. What yr. is —— in at John Lilburne Juniors (i.e. 1st, 2nd, 3rd or 4th yr.)?
    —— yr.

8. Did you have a talk with the Junior Head when —— first started?
    Yes 1
    No 2
IF YES (1) What did you talk about?
IF NO (2) Why not?

9. Did you (wife) go to the Open Day at John Lilburne Infants or Juniors this last summer?
IF YES (3) What do you remember about it?
IF NO (4) Why not?

10. Did you (wife) go to the Open Day at John Lilburne Infants or Juniors the previous summer?
IF YES (5) What do you remember about it?
IF NO (6) Why not?

11. (Apart from Open Day) have you (wife) had a talk with the Head of the Infants or Junior School at John Lilburne about —— in the last 12 months?
    Yes 1
    No 2
IF YES (1) (a) How many times?
    —— number
(b) What was the reason for your last talk?
(c) What happened then?

Questionnaire for Interviews

12. (Apart from Open Day – leaving that aside) have you had a talk with —— 's class teacher in the last 12 months?
    Yes 3
    No 4
    IF YES (3) (a) How many times?
    —— number
    (b) What was the reason for your last talk?
    (c) What happened then?
13. What is the name of ——'s class teacher now?

    _____

    Name not known 1
14. About your husband's contacts with the School. Did he go to the Open Day at John Lilburne this last summer?
    Yes 1
    No 2
    IF YES (1) What happened?
    IF NO (2) Why not?
15. Did he go to the Open Day at John Lilburne Infants or Juniors the previous summer?
    Yes 3
    No 4
    IF YES (3) What happened?
    IF NO (4) Why not?
16. (Apart from Open Day) has he had a talk with the Head of the Infants or Junior School at John Lilburne about —— in the last 12 months?
    Yes 1
    No 2
    IF YES (1) (a) How many times —— number?
    (b) What was the reason for his last talk?
    (c) What happened then?
17. (Apart from Open Day – leaving that aside) has he had a talk with ——'s class teacher in the last 12 months?
    Yes 3
    No 4
    IF YES (3) (a) How many times?
    —— number
    (b) What was the reason for his last talk?
    (c) What happened then?
18. Have either you or your husband been to any shows or concerts at John Lilburne in the last 12 months?
	Wife	Husband
Yes	1	3
No	2	4
19. If the school sent out an invitation to you and your husband to have a private talk with ——'s class teacher would either of you go?
    Yes 5
    No 6
    Undecided 7
    IF YES (5) Would you both go or only you or only your husband?
    Both 8
    Wife only 9
    Husband only 0
    (b) What would be the best time for it?

Can we just talk about the way they teach the children at John Lilburne?
20. (i) Do you know whether they teach reading much the same way as you were taught or differently?
    (ii) What about arithmetic? ⎫
    (iii) And P.T.? ⎬ CODE BELOW
    (iv) Arts and Crafts? ⎪
    (v) Other subjects? ⎭

Questionnaire for Interviews

	Reading	Arithmetic	P.T.	Arts and Crafts	Other subjects
Teach things much the same	1	4	7	0	3
Teach things differently	2	5	8	1	4
Don't know	3	6	9	2	5

ASK FOR EXAMPLES:

21. Apart from teaching methods what would you say are the main differences between John Lilburne and the school you were at when you were ——'s age?

22. If the school were to organize meetings for the parents of ——'s class to hear about teaching methods would either of you go?
    Yes 1
    No 2
    IF YES (1) (a) Would you both go or only you or only your husband?
    Both 3
    Wife only 4
    Husband only 5
    (b) What would be the best time for such a meeting at the school to start?

ASK FOR HUSBAND/WIFE AS APPLICABLE

	Husband	Wife
4.0 in the aftn.	1	1
4.30	2	2
5.00	3	3
5.30	4	4
6.00	5	5
6.30	6	6
7.00	7	7
7.30	8	8
8.00	9	9
8.30	0	0

IF NOT (2) or NOT BOTH (4 or 5) Why not? or Why wouldn't you/your husband go?

23. Are the children of the same age as —— divided into different classes now according to their ability?
    Yes 1
    No 2
    D.K. 3
    IF YES (1) How many of these classes are there in ——'s year?
    —— number

24. At any time while —— has been at John Lilburne has he/she had problems or difficulties of any kind?
    Yes 4
    No 5
    IF YES (4) (a) What were they?
    (b) Do you feel satisfied with the way the school dealt with the problem?
    Satisfied 6
    Dissatisfied 7
    Qualified 8
    Not applicable 9
    (c) In what way?

25. Do you feel that the education —— is getting is as good as, better, or worse than, most children of the same age in Britain?
    As good as 1
    Better 2
    Worse 3
    D.K. 4
    Why do you feel this way?

26. Does —— belong to a Public Library now?
    Yes 3
    No 4
    IF YES (3) Can you give me the names of any books he/she has borrowed in the last year? Anything else?
    IF NO (4) Why not?

Questionnaire for Interviews

27. Has —— borrowed any books from School during the last 12 months?
    Yes 5
    No   6
    IF YES (5) What books?

28. Has anyone bought any books for —— during the last 12 months?
    Yes 7
    No   8
    IF YES (7) (a) Who did?
        Wife   1
        Husband   2
        Other rel. 3
        Friend   4
    (b) What were they?

29. Does —— attend any clubs or other organizations not connected with the school?
    Yes 5
    No   6
    IF YES (5) (a) What clubs?
    (b) FOR FIRST CLUB RECORDED ABOVE
    How did he/she come to join in the first place?
        Child's own initiative 1
        Child's friends(s)   2
        Parent   3
        Other relative   4
        other adult   5
    IF NO (6) Why not?

30. In the evenings or at week-ends do you read to or with him/her?
    Yes 1
    No   2
    IF YES (1) Often or occasionally?
        Often   3
        Occasionally 4
    IF NO (2) Why not?

31. Do you help him/her with his/her school-work?
    Yes 5
    No   6
    IF YES (5) (a) Often or occasionally?
        Often   7
        Occasionally 8
    (b) What sort of things do you help him/her with?
    IF NO (6) Why not?

32. Apart from reading and helping with school-work in the evenings and week-ends do you play or do things with ——?
    Yes 1
    No   2
    IF YES (1) Would you say you play with him/her often or occasionally?
        Often   3
        Occasionally 4
    IF NO (2) Why not?

33. In the evenings or at week-ends does your husband read to or with him/her?
    Yes 1
    No   2
    IF YES (1) Often or occasionally?
        Often   3
        Occasionally 4
    IF NO (2) Why not?

34. Does he help him/her with his/her school-work?
    Yes 5
    No   6
    IF YES (5) (a) Often or occasionally?
        Often   7
        Occasionally 8
    (b) What sort of things does he help him/her with?
    IF NO (6) Why not?

35. Apart from reading and helping with school-work does he play or do things with —— in the evenings and week-ends?
    Yes 1
    No   2

Questionnaire for Interviews

IF YES (1) Would you say he plays with him/her often or occasionally?
    Often   3
    Occasionally   4
IF NO (2) Why not?

36. Have you or your husband talked to ―― in the last week about how he/she's getting on at school?
    Yes   1
    No   2
IF YES (1) (a) Was that you or your husband or both of you?
    Wife only   3
    Husband only   4
    Both   5
    (b) What did you talk about?

37. If there were meetings at the school on Saturday mornings would you or your husband attend?
    Yes   6
    No   7
IF YES (1) (a) Would you both go or only you or only your husband?
    Wife only   8
    Husband only   9
    Both   0
    (b) What would be the best time for such a meeting?

	Wife	Husband
9.00	1	6
9.30	2	7
10.00	3	8
10.30	4	9
11.00	5	0

38. Would you or your husband be prepared to help in making things for use in the school?
    Yes   1
    No   2

IF YES (1) (a) Would you both help or only you or your husband?
    Wife only   3
    Husband only   4
    Both   5
    (b) What sort of things would you or your husband be prepared to do?
PROBE if suggestions not forthcoming (e.g. classroom equipment, carpentry, painting, making costumes for concerts, etc.)
IF NO (2) Why not?

39. There's a possibility of making the playing space by the side of the school into a garden for the children. Would your husband be prepared to help with the work of making it into a garden?
    Yes   1
    No   2
    D.K.   3

40. Do you (wife) go out to work?
    Yes   4
    No   5
IF YES (3) (a) what is your job?
    ――――――― Occupation
    ――――――― Industry
    (b) Are your hours of work regular?
    Yes   6
    No   7
IF YES (6) (i) What time do you leave home for work?
    ――――
    (ii) What time do you arrive home from work?
    ――――
IF NO (5) What was your job before you were married?
    ――――――― Occupation
    ――――――― Industry

Questionnaire for Interviews

41. Is your husband working?
    Yes 1
    No 2
    IF YES (1) or No (2) What is/was your husband's job?
    ——————— Occupation
    ——————— Industry
42. Are his hours of work regular?
    Yes 3
    No 4
    IF YES (3) (a) What time does he leave home for work?
    ——
    (b) What time does he arrive home from work?
    ——
    IF NO (4) What sort of hours does he work?
43. At what age did you and your husband leave school?

	Wife	Husband
13 and under	1	1
14	2	2
15	3	3
16	4	4
17	5	5
18 and over	6	6
D.K.	7	7

44. Have you (wife) taken any educational course since you left school?
    Yes 1
    No 2
    IF YES (1) What kind of course?
45. Has your husband taken any educational course since he left school?
    Yes 3
    No 4
    IF YES (3) What kind of course?
46. Do you think that children at school today have a better chance than when you were at school?
    Yes 5
    No 6
    IF YES (5) In what way?
47. Are there any suggestions you would like to make about parent-teacher relations at John Lilburne?
    Yes 1
    No 2
    IF YES (1) What suggestions?
48. Is there anything you would like to know about John Lilburne that you don't know at the moment?
    Yes 3
    No 4
    IF YES (3) What would you like to know?
49. Are there any questions you would like to ask about education in general?
    Yes 5
    No 6
    IF YES (5) What do you want to know?
    NAME: ———————
    ADDRESS: ———————
    ———————
    ———————
    ———————
    DATE: ———————
    INTERVIEWER: ———————
    Present at the interview?

WIFE	all the time	1
	some of the time	2
	not present	3
	no wife	4
HUSBAND	all of the time	5
	some of the time	6
	not present	7
	no husband	8

Appendix 3
THE REGRESSION ANALYSIS

Susannah Brown and Colin Taylor

Chapter 3 mentioned the regression analysis in general terms. In this Appendix the results are given in rather more detail.

First are listed those variables which are related to the four performance variables, scores on the Verbal, Non-Verbal, Reading and Arithmetic tests. The rest of the variables, derived from the questions as printed in Appendix 2, were divided for the purpose of analysis into the following categories:

    Family Background variables: 5–27
    Parental Interest variables: 28–65
    Age: 66

The scores on each variable were obtained by ranking the answers to the questions.

LIST OF VARIABLES IN REGRESSION ANALYSIS

1. Child's Verbal I.Q.
2. Child's Non-Verbal I.Q.
3. Child's Reading score
4. Child's Arithmetic score
5. Length of residence in neighbourhood
6. Mother's birthplace
7. Whether mother immigrant or not
8. Father's birthplace
9. Family size
10. (Family size)^2

The Regression Analysis

11. Position of subject in household
12. Only child or not
13. Siblings of pre-school age
14. Siblings of primary school age
15. Mother's age
16. Whether subject has father in household
17. Father's age
18. Number of adults in household
19. Whether child attended John Lilburne Infants
20. Mother's occupation
21. Mother's hours of employment
22. Father's occupation
23. Father's hours of employment
24. Mother's school leaving age
25. Father's school leaving age
26. Mother's post-school education
27. Father's post-school education
28. Parent spoke to Infants Head when child first started
29. Parent spoke to Juniors Head when child first started
30. Mother went to 1965 Open Day
31. Mother went to 1964 Open Day
32. Mother spoke to Head in previous 12 months
33. Mother spoke to teacher in previous 12 months
34. Father went to 1965 Open Day
35. Father went to 1964 Open Day
36. Father spoke to Head in previous 12 months
37. Father spoke to teacher in previous 12 months
38. Parents attended concerts or shows
39. Willingness to have private talk with teacher
40. Willingness to attend meetings about teaching methods
41. Willingness to attend Saturday morning meetings
42. Father prepared to convert playing fields
43. Parent has suggestion about P/T relations
44. Parent would like to know more about John Lilburne
45. Informant would like to know about education
46. Knowledge of child's year
47. Knowledge of class teacher's name

The Regression Analysis

48. Parent believes reading is taught differently
49. Parent believes arithmetic taught differently
50. Parent believes P.E. taught differently
51. Parent believes Arts and Crafts taught differently
52. Parent believes other subjects taught differently
53. Knowledge about streaming
54. Child's membership of Public Library
55. Child borrows books from school library
56. Books bought for child
57. Child belongs to clubs
58. Child joins clubs on parents' initiative
59. Mother reads to child
60. Mother helps child with school-work
61. Mother plays with child
62. Father reads to child
63. Father helps child with school-work
64. Father plays with child
65. Either parent talked to child about school in previous week
66. Age of child on 1.5.65

At the beginning two principal component analyses were made, one on a group of variables pertaining to contact with the school (variables 28 to 42), the other to variables which show knowledge of the school and encouragement in the home (variables 43 to 65). This was done in order to discover whether some of these original questions could be properly grouped rather than all being considered individually at subsequent stages. This did not turn out to be so. The first principal component on contacts with the school accounted for only 22 per cent of the variability of the original variables, and the first component on knowledge of the school and encouragement in the home for only 13 per cent.

The next stage was to carry out a regression analysis based on the interviews. In the following tables the results are

The Regression Analysis

given separately for each of the four performance tests. Tables 1 relate performance to the Parental Interest variables alone, with age of child held constant. Age was considered just in case it turned out to be closely related to performance. If the older children had done consistently and markedly better the tests would not have been properly standardized for our purpose. Any improvement in performance between the 1st and 2nd phases would then probably have been due more than anything else merely to the fact that the children were six months older. Fortunately, age was not significantly correlated with performance.

Tables 2 relate performance to the same Parental Interest variables but with Family Background variables held constant as well as age of child. The point was to see whether the same type of variables still appeared as significant when allowance was made for features of the family background like occupational class and size of family. Tables 3 relate performance to both Parental Interest and Family Background variables.

The computer programme used a stepwise regression analysis. This was a way of reducing the variables to a manageable number. Performance was first regressed on age (Tables 1) or on age and family background (Tables 2) and then the variable was introduced into the analysis which in addition correlated most highly with performance. The next variable to be introduced was the one which correlated most highly with performance after those already in the regression had been taken into account. Variables were thus introduced one at a time until the addition of a further variable was not significant at the 10 per cent level. The variables appear in the tables in the order in which they were introduced.

Where a particular variable which appears in one table does not in another it means that it was statistically significant in the one but not in the other. One would not expect all the same variables to appear in the different sets of tables because the introduction of the Family Background variables would almost inevitably affect the weight of some

The Regression Analysis

of the different Parental Interest Variables, and the performance of children was not the same on the different tests.

The main conclusions which can be drawn from these tables have been stated in Chapter 3, i.e. in general they support the Plowden findings about the importance of Parental Interest; they indicate to some extent the relative importance of the different variables or types of variables (particularly membership of a library), and they point to some negative correlations of interest.

TABLE 1.1

RELATIONSHIP BETWEEN SCORES OF CHILDREN ON VERBAL INTELLIGENCE TESTS AND PARENTAL INTEREST WITH AGE OF CHILD HELD CONSTANT

Variable	Standardized Regression Coefficient b	Simple Correlation r	Percentage contribution to variance $100\,br$
Age (NS)	0·007	0·173	0·13
Child's membership of Public Library	0·382	0·424	16·16
Parents attended concerts or shows	0·206	0·384	7·89
Knowledge of child's year	0·278	0·346	9·60
Father reads to child	−0·238	−0·207	4·91
Mother plays with child	0·207	0·268	5·53
Father went to 1965 Open Day	0·202	0·344	6·95
Child belongs to clubs	0·152	0·276	4·19
Father plays with child	−0·180	0·072	−1·30
Father prepared to convert playing field NS	0·140	0·171	2·39
Father spoke to teacher in previous 12 months NS	−0·116	0·067	−0·78

Total percentage of variance in Verbal IQ attributed to Parental Interest and Age = 55·7%

Variables marked NS were significant at the 10% level all the time they were introduced but not at the 5% level. All other variables were significant at the 5% level all the time they were introduced.

For convenience, the significance tests for this and other tables used the ordinary F distribution throughout.

148

The Regression Analysis

TABLE 1.2
RELATIONSHIP BETWEEN SCORES OF CHILDREN ON NON-VERBAL INTELLIGENCE TESTS AND PARENTAL INTEREST WITH AGE OF CHILD HELD CONSTANT

Variable	Standardized Regression Coefficient b	Simple Correlation r	Percentage contribution to variance $100\,br$
Age (NS)	—0·001	0·070	—0·01
Parents attended concerts or shows	0·184	0·336	6·17
Child's membership of Public Library	0·293	0·339	9·93
Knowledge of child's year	0·202	0·280	5·65
Father plays with child	—0·260	—0·081	2·10
Father went to 1965 Open Day	0·233	0·310	7·21
Child joins club on parent's initiative	0·166	0·255	4·22

Total percentage of variance in Non-Verbal IQ attributed to Parental Interest and Age = 35·3%.

All variables were significant at the 5% level at the time they were introduced.

The Regression Analysis

TABLE 1.3

RELATIONSHIP BETWEEN SCORES OF CHILDREN ON READING TESTS AND PARENTAL INTEREST VARIABLES WITH AGE OF CHILD HELD CONSTANT

Variable	Standardized Regression Coefficient b	Simple Correlation r	Percentage contribution to variance $100\,br$
Age (NS)	−0·108	0·027	−0·29
Parents attended shows or concerts	0·222	0·420	9·33
Child's membership of Public Library	0·287	0·362	10·38
Knowledge of child's year	0·272	0·383	10·44
Mother reads to child	−0·157	−0·127	1·99
Mother plays with child	0·209	0·266	5·55
Father reads to child	−0·251	−0·200	5·03
Father went to 1965 Open Day	0·151	0·356	5·38
Mother went to 1965 Open Day NS	0·147	0·356	5·23

Total percentage of variance in Reading Ability attributed to Parental Interest and Age = 53·0%.

Variables marked NS were significant at the 10% level at the time these were introduced but not at the 5% level. All other variables were significant at the 5% level at the time they were introduced.

The Regression Analysis

Table 1.4
Relationship between Scores of Children on Arithmetic Tests and Parental Interest Variables with Age of Child held Constant

Variable	Standardized Regression Coefficient *b*	Simple Correlation *r*	Percentage contribution to variance 100 *br*
Age (NS)	−0·049	0·063	−0·31
Child's membership of Public Library	0·358	0·371	13·26
Father went to 1965 Open Day	0·296	0·370	10·94
Parents attended shows or concerts	0·301	0·345	10·36
Knowledge of child's year	0·199	0·256	5·10
Child borrows books from school library NS	0·179	0·091	1·62
Father plays with child NS	−0·215	0·034	−0·72
Father prepared to convert playing field NS	0·180	0·175	3·15
Father spoken to teacher in previous 12 months NS	−0·163	0·004	−0·07
Mother went to 1965 Open Day NS	−0·163	0·136	−2·22

Total percentage of variance in Arithmetic Ability attributed to Parental Interest and Age = 41·1%.

Variables marked NS were significant at the 10% level at the time they were introduced but not at the 5% level. All other variables were significant at the 5% level at the time they were introduced.

The Regression Analysis

TABLE 2.1

RELATIONSHIP BETWEEN SCORES OF CHILDREN ON VERBAL INTELLIGENCE TESTS AND PARENTAL INTEREST WITH FAMILY BACKGROUND AND AGE OF CHILD HELD CONSTANT

Variable	Standardized Regression Coefficient b	Simple Correlation r	Percentage contribution to variance $100\, br$
Family background and age	—	—	37·87
Knowledge of child's year	0·284	0·346	9·75
Father reads to child	—0·222	—0·207	4·58
Mother plays with child	0·196	0·268	5·25
Child's membership of Public Library	0·192	0·424	8·13
Parents attended concerts or shows NS	0·131	0·384	5·02

Total percentage of variance in Verbal IQ attributed to Parental Interest, Family Background and Age = 70·6%.

Variables marked NS were significant at the 10% level at the time they were introduced but not at the 5% level. All other variables were significant at the 5% level at the time they were introduced.

The Regression Analysis

TABLE 2.2

RELATIONSHIP BETWEEN SCORES OF CHILDREN ON NON-VERBAL INTELLIGENCE TESTS AND PARENTAL INTEREST WITH FAMILY BACKGROUND AND AGE OF CHILD HELD CONSTANT

Variable	Standardized Regressions Coefficient b	Simple Correlation r	Percentage contribution to variance $100\,br$
Family background and age	—	—	32·84
Knowledge of child's year	0·241	0·280	6·74
Parents spoke to Junior Head when child started NS	−0·182	−0·200	3·65
Mother reads to child NS	−0·162	−0·070	1·14

Total percentage of variance in Non-Verbal IQ attributed to Parental Interest, Family Background and Age = 44·4%.

Variables marked NS were significant at the 10% level at the time they were introduced but not at the 5% level. All other variables were significant at the 5% level at the time they were introduced.

The Regression Analysis

TABLE 2.3

RELATIONSHIP BETWEEN SCORES OF CHILDREN ON READING TESTS AND PARENTAL INTEREST WITH FAMILY BACKGROUND AND AGE OF CHILD HELD CONSTANT

Variable	Standardized Regression Coefficient b	Simple Correlation r	Percentage contribution to variance $100\,br$
Family background and age	—	—	28·90
Knowledge of child's year	0·291	0·383	11·15
Father reads to child	−0·193	−0·200	3·86
Mother plays with child	0·200	0·266	5·31
Parents attended concerts or shows	0·193	0·420	8·09
Mother reads to child NS	−0·189	−0·127	2·39
Father spoke to Head in previous 12 months	−0·143	0·008	−0·12
Child's membership of Public Library NS	0·144	0·362	5·21

Total percentage of variance in Reading attributed to Parental Interest, Family Background and Age = 64·8%.

Variables marked NS were significant at the 10% level at the time they were introduced but not at the 5% level. All other variables were significant at the 5% level at the time they were introduced.

The Regression Analysis

TABLE 2·4
RELATIONSHIP BETWEEN SCORES OF CHILDREN ON ARITHMETIC TESTS AND PARENTAL INTEREST WITH FAMILY BACKGROUND AND AGE OF CHILD HELD CONSTANT

Variable	Standardized Regression Coefficient b	Simple Correlation r	Percentage contribution to variance $100\,br$
Family background and age	—	—	29·46
Father went to 1965 Open Day	0·272	0·370	10·05
Parent believes reading is taught differently NS	−0·161	−0·031	0·51

Total percentage of variance in Arithmetic Ability attributed to Parental Interest, Family Background and Age = 40·0%.

Variables marked NS were significant at the 10% level at the time they were introduced but not at the 5% level. All the other variables were significant at the 5% level at the time they were introduced.

The Regression Analysis

TABLE 3.1

RELATIONSHIP BETWEEN SCORES OF CHILDREN ON VERBAL INTELLIGENCE TESTS AND PARENTAL INTEREST AND FAMILY BACKGROUND

Variable	Standardized Regression Coefficient b	Simple Correlation r	Percentage contribution to variance $100\,br$
Father's post-school education	0·160	0·433	6·93
Knowledge of child's year	0·270	0·346	9·32
Child's membership of Public Library	0·205	0·424	8·69
Mother plays with child	0·216	0·268	5·79
Father plays with child	−0·277	−0·207	5·72
Father's occupation	0·230	0·338	7·78
Mother's post-school education	0·222	0·380	8·45
Mother's age	0·183	0·183	3·34
Subject has father in household	0·183	0·176	3·23
Parents attended school concerts or shows	0·142	0·384	5·43
Parent has suggestion about P/T relations	−0·139	0·086	−1·19
Child belongs to club NS	0·125	0·276	3·44
Parent believes Arithmetic taught differently	0·121	0·144	1·74

Total percentage of variance of Verbal IQ attributed to Parental Interest together with Family Background = 68·7%.

Variables marked NS were significant at the 10% level at the time they were introduced but not at the 5% level. All other variables were significant at the 5% level at the time they were introduced.

The Regression Analysis

TABLE 3.2

RELATIONSHIP BETWEEN SCORES OF CHILDREN ON NON-VERBAL INTELLIGENCE TESTS AND PARENTAL INTEREST AND FAMILY BACKGROUND

Variable	Standardized Regression Coefficient b	Simple Correlation r	Percentage contribution to variance $100\,br$
Mother's post school education	0·325	0·351	11·41
Child's membership of Public Library	0·240	0·339	8·13
Parents attended concerts or shows	0·138	0·336	4·63
Knowledge of child's year	0·241	0·280	6·76
Father plays with child	−0·230	−0·081	1·86
Father went to 1965 Open Day	0·191	0·310	5·91
Parents spoke to Juniors Head when child first started	−0·155	−0·200	3·11
Mother reads to child NS	−0·173	−0·070	1·22
Child joined club on parents initiative NS	−0·203	−0·255	5·17
Mother attended 1964 Open Day NS	−0·196	0·119	−2·33
Parent believes arithmetic taught differently NS	0·141	0·144	2·04
Willingness to attend meetings about teaching NS	−0·165	0·024	−0·39
Mother plays with child NS	0·154	0·109	1·68
Knowledge about streaming NS	0·125	0·146	1·82

Total percentage of variance in Non-Verbal IQ attributed to Parental Interest together with Family Background = 51·0%.

Variables marked NS were significant at the 10% level at the time they were introduced but not at the 5% level. All other variables were significant at the 5% level at the time they were introduced.

The Regression Analysis

TABLE 3.3

RELATIONSHIP BETWEEN SCORES OF CHILDREN ON READING TESTS AND PARENTAL INTEREST AND FAMILY BACKGROUND

Variable	Standardized Regression Coefficient b	Simple Correlation r	Percentage contribution to variance $100\,br$
Father's post-school education	0·195	0·440	8·58
Knowledge of child's year	0·301	0·383	11·53
Parents attended shows or concerts	0·218	0·420	9·16
Mother reads to child	—0·206	—0·127	2·60
Mother plays with child	0·248	0·266	6·60
Mother's post-school education	0·215	0·357	7·68
Child's membership of Public Library	0·161	0·362	5·83
Father reads to child	—0·196	—0·200	3·93
Father's occupation	0·183	0·307	5·62
Father spoke to Head in previous 12 months NS	—0·114	0·008	—0·10

Total percentage of variance in Reading Ability attributed to Parental Interest together with Family background = 61·4%.

Variables marked NS were significant at the 10% level at the time they were introduced but not at the 5% level. All other variables were significant at the 5% level at the time they were introduced.

The Regression Analysis

TABLE 3.4
RELATIONSHIP BETWEEN SCORES OF CHILDREN ON ARITHMETIC TESTS AND PARENTAL INTEREST AND FAMILY BACKGROUND

Variable	Standardized Regression Coefficient b	Simple Correlation r	Percentage contribution to variance $100\,br$
Child's membership of Public Library	0.234	0.371	8.68
Father went to 1965 Open Day	0.202	0.370	7.49
Parents attended shows or concerts	0.232	0.345	8.00
Mother's post school education	0.240	0.332	7.96
Father's occupation NS	0.165	0.263	4.33
Books bought for child NS	−0.255	0.048	−1.22
Knowledge of child's year	0.210	0.256	5.39
Father prepared to convert playing field NS	0.234	0.175	4.11
Willingness to attend meetings about teaching methods	−0.213	0.061	−1.30
Father spoke to teacher in previous 12 months NS	−0.130	0.004	−0.06
Parent believes reading is taught differently NS	−0.178	−0.031	0.56
Length of residence in neighbourhood NS	0.151	0.248	3.75
Parent believes arts and crafts taught differently NS	0.142	0.082	1.17

Total percentage of variance in Arithmetic Ability attributed to Parental Interest together with Family background = 48.9%.

Variables marked NS were significant at the 10% level at the time they were introduced but not at the 5% level. All other variables were significant at the 5% level at the time they were introduced.

Appendix 4
LIST OF REFERENCES

BERNSTEIN, B., 'Social Class and Linguistic Development'. In Halsey, A. H., Floud, J., and Anderson, C. A., *Education, Economy and Society*. New York, The Free Press of Glencoe. 1961.

BOOTH, C., *Life and Labour of the People in London*. 17 vols. First Series: Poverty, Vol. 3. London, Macmillan. 1902.

BURGIN, T., and EDSON, P. *Spring Grove – The Education of Immigrant Children*. Oxford University Press. 1967.

BURT, C., *The Backward Child*. London, University of London Press. 1951.

CENTRAL ADVISORY COUNCIL FOR EDUCATION, *Children and Their Primary Schools* (Plowden Report). London, H.M.S.O. 1967.

CENTRAL ADVISORY COUNCIL FOR EDUCATION, *Half Our Future* (Newsom Report). London, H.M.S.O. 1963.

CHORLTON, A. R., 'Attaching Social Workers to Schools'. See Craft, M., Raynor, J. and Cohen, L.

CONSULTATIVE COMMITTEE ON THE PRIMARY SCHOOL (Hadow Report). London, H.M.S.O. 1931.

CRAFT, M., RAYNOR, J., and COHEN, L., *Linking Home and School*, London, Longmans. 1967.

DOBBS, A. E., *Education and Social Movements 1700–1850*. London. 1919.

DOUGLAS, J. W. B., *The Home and the School*. London, MacGibbon and Kee. 1964.

DOWNING, J., *The I.T.A. Symposium*. London, National Foundation for Educational Research. 1967.

List of References

FRASER, E., *Home Environment and the School*. London, University of London Press. 1959.
GLASS, R. (ed.), *The Social Background of a Plan: A Survey of Middlesbrough*. Routledge and Kegan Paul. 1948.
GRANT, N., *Soviet Education*. London, Penguin. 1964.
GREEN, L., *Parents and Teachers—Partners or Rivals?* Allen and Unwin, 1968.
ILLINGWORTH, R. S. and ILLINGWORTH, C. M., *Lessons from Childhood*. Edinburgh, Livingstone. 1966.
KATZ, E. and LAZARSFELD, P. F., *Personal Influence*. Illinois, The Free Press of Glencoe. 1955.
KLAPPER, J. T., *The Effects of Mass Communication*. Illinois, The Free Press of Glencoe. 1960.
LAZARSFELD, P. F. and others, *The People's Choice*. 2nd ed. Illinois, The Free Press of Glencoe. New York, Columbia University Press. 1948.
LONDON COUNCIL OF SOCIAL SERVICE, *The Young Immigrant at Home and at School*. Report of Day Conference. 1964.
MAGARSHACK, D. *Chekhov the Dramatist*, London, MacGibbon and Kee. 1960.
MAYO, E., *The Human Problems of an Industrial Civilization*. New York, MacMillan. 1933.
MAYS, J. B., *Education and the Urban Child*. Liverpool, Liverpool University Press. 1962.
MUSGRAVE, P. W., *The Sociology of Education*. London, Methuen. 1965.
ROBSON, E. R., *School Architecture*. London, John Murray. 1874.
SPALDING, T. A., *The Work of the London School Board*. London. 1900.
TROPP, A. *The Teachers*. London Heinemann. 1957.
WALL, W. D., 'The Opinions of Teachers on Parent-Teacher Co-operation'. *British Journal of Educational Psychology*, Vol. 17. 1947.
WATTS, A. F., PIDGEON, D. A. and YATES, A., *Secondary School Entrance Examinations*. London, Newnes. 1952.

List of References

WYLIE, L., *Village in the Vaucluse*. Harvard University Press. 1961.

YOUNG, M. and ARMSTRONG, M., *The Flexible School*. Advisory Centre for Education (ACE), *Where?* Autumn 1965, Supplement 5.

YOUNG, M., *Innovation and Research in Education*. London, Routledge and Kegan Paul. 1965.

YOUNG, M., 'Parent-Teacher Co-operation'. See Craft, M., Raynor, J. and Cohen, L.

INDEX

Advisory Centre for Education (A.C.E.), 115
Anderson, C. A., 8
Annual reports on pupils, 19, 66
Arithmetic, methods of teaching, 32
  meeting for discussion of, 57–8, 99
Arnold, Matthew, 112
Arts and crafts, discussion on, 56, 58–9, 65

Backward children, 20, 126–7
Bank Street Primary School, immigrants at, 68–9
Bernstein, Basil, 8
Bethnal Green Effect, 94
Boarding schools, private, 111–12
Books, importance of, 31, 36–7, 49, 59, 100–2
Booth, Charles, 1, 117
Burgin, T., 86
Burt, Sir Cyril, 6, 126–7

Cambridge House, Camberwell, 86
Cars, 117
Central Advisory Council for Education, Reports of, *see under* name of chairman, e.g. Plowden, Newsom
Certificate of Secondary Education (C.S.E.), 113
Chekhov, Anton, 36, 58
Chorlton, A. R., 124
Cinema, 117
Co-education, immigrants' objection to, 78, 80
Cohen, L., 124
Confederation for the Advancement of State Education (C.A.S.E.), 115

Craft, M., 124
Crowther Report, 6
Curriculum, vii, 28, 74

Discipline, school, 27, 79, 111
Dobbs, A. E., 117
Do-it-yourself, 117
Douglas, J. W. B., 6, 7
Downing, J., 10

Edge Hill College of Education, 125
Edson, P., 86
Education Visitors, 124–5
Educational background,
  of immigrants, 25, 74–7, 86
  of other parents, 25–7
Educational Priority Areas, 4, 5, 7, 130
Educational Welfare Officers, 125
Encyclopaedias, 31

Family, changing structure of, 116–19
Fathers,
  helping with arithmetic, 32
  hours of work, 42–3, 85
  immigrant, 72, 73, 77, 85
  number at Open Meetings, 51
  number at discussions on teaching methods, 57, 58
  see also Parents
Floud, J., 8
Fraser, E., 6

Glasgow, 124
Glass, R., 6
Grant, N., 109
Green, L., 122

Index

Hadow Report, 28, 35, 112
Halsey, A. H., 8
Hawthorne Effect, 94
Headmaster,
  and immigrants' problems, 78-85
  open letter to parents, 48-50, 57, 66, 80
  support for trial programme, 55, 65-6
  sympathetic to parents, 43
  talks with parents, 15-17
  typical day, 44-5
H.M.I.s, 126
Home and School Council, 115
Home and School Research Association, 127
Home environment,
  effect on educational progress, vi-viii, 6-9, 34-41, 97-106 pass., 117-19
  of immigrants, 67-86
Homework,
  new approach to, 121-2
  parents want, 28, 74-5, 80
Housing conditions,
  affecting school performance, 6-7
  described, 60-3 pass.
  immigrants', 4, 67-86 pass.
  substandard, 3

Immigrants, 4, 25, 67-86
  educational background of, 74-5
  encouragement of children, 75-7
  English classes for, 85-6
  families described, 81-4
  home visits to, 80
  housing conditions, 70-1, 84-6 pass.
  ignorance of school, 71-4, 86
  language barriers, 71-3, 80
  letters translated, 48, 80
  long hours worked, 85
  number visiting school, 79
  pupils' score in performance tests, 96
  special meetings for, 79-80
  uprootedness, 77-8
Immigrant liaison officers needed, 86

Industrial Revolution, 117
Initial Teaching Alphabet (I.T.A.), 10, 87

Katz, E., 8
Klapper, J. T., 9

Lazarsfeld, P. F., 8, 9
Libraries,
  public, 31, 37, 40, 48, 51, 59, 100
  school, 31, 52
London Council of Social Service, 75, 77
London School Board, 1, 2

McGeeney, P., 11, 119, 127
Magarshack, D., 36
Mark Hendon Primary School,
  immigrants at, 67-8
Mayo, E., 94
Mays, J. B., 123
Mothers,
  helping with reading, 32
  immigrant, 68, 72, 80, 81, 85
  number at Open Day, 18
  number at Open Meeting, 51
  number at discussions on teaching methods, 57, 58
  number having talks with teachers and Head, 15-18
  number taking children to school on first day, 13-14
  working, 4, 43
  see also parents
Musgrave, P. W., 114

National Federation of Parent-Teacher Associations, 115
Newsom Report, 5, 6
Nuffield Foundation, 9

Open Day, 18-21
Open Meetings, 50-53
Oxfordshire, Director of Education for, 124

Parent Participation in schools, 97-106 pass., 107-30 pass.

Index

Parent Participation in schools – *continued*
and effect on children's performance, 6–11 *pass.*, 34–41, 97–106 *pass.*, 144–59
at Open Day, 18–22
at Open Meetings, 50–3
closer link proposed, vi–vii, 4–6
exchange of information about, 127–30
increase in likely, 115–30, *pass.*
in discussion on teaching methods, 56–9, 64–6, 79
in other countries, 108–11
lack of in England. 108–12 *pass.*
new practice in, 119–30 *pass.*
teachers' attitude to, 64–6, 108
Parent-Teacher Associations (P.T.A.s), 21, 110, 120
Parents,
absentee, 59, 123–5
attitudes to school, 23–41
case-studies, 99–106
choice of school, 14–15
contacts with school, 13–22
criticism of school, 20–2, 27–9
discussions on teaching methods, 56–9, 64, 65
encouragement and children's progress, 6–11 *pass.*, 34–41, 97–106 *pass.*
home visits to, 59–63
hours of work, 42–3
housing, 6
ignorance of school, 32–4
income, 6
interest in education, vi-viii, 6–8, 25–7, 33–4, 118–19, 127–30
occupations, 4, 6
Open Letter to, 48–50, 57, 66
questionnaire used with, 37, 137–43
talks with teachers, 53–5, 64, 65, 98–9
teaching methods, knowledge of, 29–34
see also immigrants
Parker, G., 38

Pastoral care of pupils, 111–12
Pidgeon, D. A., 90, 133
Plowden Report, 4, 5, 6, 7, 10, 11, 28, 30, 39, 63, 108, 110, 119, 121, 148

Questionnaire put to parents, 37, 137–43

Raynor, J., 124
Reading, methods of teaching, 29–31
meeting for discussion, 56, 99–100
Regression analysis, 38–9, 144–59
Robbins Report, 6
Robson, E. R., 2

Schonell and Adams Intelligence Test, 132
School architecture, 1–3
School play, 21
Schoolkeeper, 47
Smith R., 2
Spring Grove School, Huddersfield, 86
Streaming, 33
Stuart, J. E., 132
Surrey Educational Research Association, 127

Teachers,
and trial programme, 50–66, *pass.*
attitude to parents, 44, 47, 64–6
classroom autonomy of, 112–14
discipline, 72, 79, 111
friendliness to children, 24, 27
home visits to pupils, 59, 63
informal contact with parents, 15, 17–18
met at Open Day, 18–22
met at Open Meetings, 50–53
opposition to parent participation, 107–30 *pass.*
private talks, attitude to, 53–5, 64
professional status, 114
teaching method discussions, attitude to 55–9, 64–6
Teaching methods,
discussions on, 56–9, 64, 65–6

Index

Teaching methods – *continued*
  parents' awareness of, 29
  parents' need to learn about, 120–1, 129
Tests of educational performance, vii, 87–106, 131–6
  arithmetic attainment test, 133–4
  arithmetic score, 97
  at Fenton School, 92–5
  at Thorne School, 92–5
  changes in score, 88–91
  conditions for 135–6
  'control' schools added, 91–3
  criteria for selection, 131–2
  effects of practice in, 90–1, 93, 94, 105
  immigrant performance in, 96
  improved teaching after, 93–4
  non-verbal intelligence test, 88–91, 132–3
  parents and, 37–41, 97–106 *pass*.
  reading attainment test, 133
  regression analysis and, 38–9, 144–59
  validity of, 134
  verbal intelligence test, 88–9, 96, 132
Tropp, A., 114

Watts, A. F., 90, 133
Wylie, L., 109

Yates, A., 90
The Young Immigrant at Home and at School, 75, 77
Young, M., 6, 10, 124

Printed in the United States
by Baker & Taylor Publisher Services